Table of Contents

Introduction – Pages 2 - 7

Chp. I – I Beat the Odds – Page 8 - 21

Chp. II – The Kitchen – Pages – 21 - 35

Chp III – My Smile – Pages 35 - 62

Chp. IV - Food or Alcohol – Pages 63 - 83

Chp. V – Hunger? Pages 84 - 95

Chp. VI – The Seizures – Pages 119- 131

Chp. VII– The Burn – Pages 131 - 164

Chp. VIII– Big & Botly (Fat) – Pages - 164 - 173

Chp IX - Soundtracks of My Childhood – 174 - 190

Chp X – Successfully Surviving the Monster 174 –

Introduction

Beating the odds started in childhood; I grew up dirt poor in Greenville, Mississippi in the home of an explosive single mother who was an emotionally unbalanced alcohol and drug addict. She tortured and abused me from the day I was born, until the day she died. Although my siblings were abused to some degree, I received the brunt of her abuse. It is often said that she singled me out. She systematically isolated us from family, friends and the community; so she could destroy us.

I broke my family legacy of alcohol and drug addiction, abuse and destructive patterns of behaviors. I have changed my family legacy by creating a new family legacy through my three children. Yet, I am facing and beating my odds because I became a fighter, survivor and soldier.

Today, I beat the odds. I am successfully surviving the monster, which was my mom. I am living proof that beating the odds is a process not an event. Every day I am taking this journey. I am determined and committed to be a successful survivor. I have three godly, educated, successful and well balanced young adult children. I have obtained a Bachelor's degree in Psychology and a Master's degree in Counseling. In spite of the monster I possess a peace from God that has passed all my understanding.

I Beat the Odds' is my story as a successful survivor of torture and abuse at the hands of my mother. Today is July 3, 2013. I am homeless and for many months my three children and I lived in a U-Haul. Many of life's necessities I do not own such as a home, car, bed to sleep in or money in the bank. I have not had regular employment since March 25,

2008 and the odds are still stacked against me; but I am a prepared writer and business owner. However, I am a successful survivor.

As challenging and difficult as my present circumstances are; my childhood was much worse. I realize now that my childhood tragedies were to help prepare me to be "strong enough to deal with the problems of others as well as my present circumstances. Today I realize that childhood is only preparation for adulthood. My life experiences afford me the focus, discipline, perseverance and ability to write about my amazing journey. As you read you will run through a scale of emotions from sadness, anger, exhaustion, but my hope is that you will be inspired, motivated and empowered. It will remind, inform and reassure you that no matter your circumstances, you can successfully rise above them, if you want too. As you read I encourage you to do an introspective

4

examination to determine if you are living a life of success or failure. You will understand that success is in the eyes of the beholder, because success to one person is not success to the next person.

You will learn that your circumstances have only as much power over you, as you allow them to have. Circumstances are those influences from the people, places and things that surround you; it is your decision how you handle and respond to them. It is up to each individual to determine whether your circumstances will make you or break you. Your circumstances will drive you to succeed or fail. The outcome depends on whether you want to rise above them (succeed) or fall victim to them (fail). **Falling victim** to your circumstances is played out when the victim becomes the victimizer and repeats the same destructive patterns of behavior. **Rising above** your circumstances is demonstrated when a victim **fights** through, **survives** the worse to become a real **soldier** in order to **inspire, motivate** and **empower** others to rise above their circumstances.

This book is a testament to my journey from victim to victor. My journey has been filled with obstacles; which caused me to take many detours; there were lots of bumps in the road; had several warnings; countless roadblocks and endless stops and starts. But in spite of all these obstacles, I am a successful survivor. I am committed and determined to complete this journey in a positive way.

My life has been filled with many peaks (good days) and valleys (dark days). I will be the first to admit that there have been many more valleys than peaks in my life. But I will also admit that I am better because of my valley days. I believed if it was not for the valleys, I would not have made it this far. **I beat the odds,**

because my peaks were few, but my valleys have been endless. Torture, abuse and tragedy did not break or destroy me, but drove me to success. Success for me is continuing to beat the odds.

Peaks and Valleys; success or failure; ups and downs; it does not matter, I still have hope in God and I thank God that he gave me sanity in the face of so much insanity. Because all the odds were stacked against me; I am determine to be a successful survivor. The countless valley days pushed me to conduct various workshops; motivational and public speaking; executive and life coaching. I was able to teach and train individuals how to be motivated, inspired and empowered, in spite of your circumstances.

Chapter 1 - I Beat the Odds

October 26, 1998, the morning of mom's death, she called me intoxicated. My phone rang early that morning, I was rushing and on my way to work, but I picked it up, because I figured it was her. I could hear short shallow breathing (from over 40 years of cigarette smoking) and profanities coming through the phone. She was demanding that I go buy her some alcohol and cigarettes. I refused, so the breathing and profanities intensified. She hung up the phone, but called right back, so I did not pick it up. Mom spent her life, her energy and time doing and saying everything she could to break and destroy my spirit. A few hours later, she died the way she lived; intoxicated, abusive and bitter.

For thirty-two years mom said, "Faye, I hate you and all my children, because y'all stole my youth from me.

You were not worth the sex it took to get you here. I never wanted to have any children. I was just having sex to get money." She spit, beat, and burned me as often as she could. Every memory of mom is a negative one. I have searched my mind from one memory to the next, but all I have are terrible thoughts of the monster, called mom. To the neighbors she was a beautiful, well dressed, kind, thoughtful and hard working mother of ten. But to me, she was a monster, who tortured and abused me for thirty two years.

Beating the odds has been and continues to be a life long journey for me. I am determined to rise above the terrible circumstances of my abusive childhood. In order to beat the odds every day I commit and re-commit to ensure my abuser doesn't win. As a helpless child, many days I longed and prayed for someone to come and stop her from abusing me. I

9

wish someone would have said, "Celeste do not torture and mistreat Faye", but it never happened. Mom was the irresponsible adult, who abused me, but now I am the adult; I decided to be responsible, make better decisions and be a positive resource for others who may need to know how to rise above their negative circumstances. I am determined and committed to help the helpless: to empower the powerless; to educate the uneducated in the ways that makes their lives successful. Because no one helped us, I am compelled to help whoever I can. I am determined to leave a better family legacy and break the pattern of destructive behaviors in my family. My story will show, "I Beat the Odds". I want victims and survivors to know how I did it and show them how to "beat their odds", no matter what those odds may be. I am offering this book to anyone who is searching for hope, especially in the face of hopelessness. The odds I beat include torture, sexual and physical abuse, violence, a family cycle and pattern of alcohol and drug addiction, poverty, single parenthood, broken home, racism and many other negative circumstances. I knew as a young child that it was not right or acceptable for parents to torture, abuse, and bully their children. I was young, innocent and helpless, but that made me more vulnerable to mom. I always knew the way I was treated was wrong, but I did not know how to get out or how to avoid her abuse. I also knew it was wrong for my older siblings, family, adult neighbors and the police to ignore my pain and turn a deaf ear. Most of my childhood experiences are difficult to re-call, re-live, as well as to share. It will be hard for most readers to wade through. As challenging as it will be to read it is one of the hardest undertakings of my life. I find it emotionally agonizing, but therapeutic to re-live and write about it. The most difficult thing about successfully surviving is that it requires the survivor to work every day. This book is about BEING A FIGHTER, SURVIVOR & SOLDIER, WHO BEAT THE ODDS.

The bible says, "So a man thinks in his heart so is he". As a child without realizing it, I had to think of myself as a winner. Mom did everything within her power to destroy me and break my spirit. She worked extra hard to convince me that I was a loser. I learned "If you think you are defeated than you are defeated". I never thought I was defeated and I knew quitting was never an option. I knew if I quit, it was over and I would never get to the other side of my pain. It is only by God's grace and his goodness that "I beat those odds". I grew up with ten siblings today nine are alcoholics and addicts. Beating the odds has always been my determination.

I realize now that many of my childhood neighbors, my community and the police who ignored my pain and the police empowered my mother. When they did not help me, they silently accepted and gave permission to my abuser. They did nothing to stop her, so she inflicted more pain on me. My story is intended to reach the victim and victimizer. I want to encourage and motivate survivors of torture, violence and all negative circumstances that there is hope. I want them to learn how to stand up and say no to their abuser. Inspire victims and survivors to learn how to love, accept and feel good about themselves, is what I hope to achieve. I want you to know that you are and can continue to be a strong, bold and a successful survivor. I want victims and survivors to know the worst is behind and if you accept that, then your best is in front of you. Like mom and many of my relatives I could have given up and drowned in self-pity, but I always wanted to change my family legacy for my children and create new patterns and behaviors. God blessed and gave me a different insight which has helped me to know early on that I was different. This insight made me a fighter; survivor and a soldier, so I could beat the odds. As a young child, I knew the odds of surviving my mother's home were stacked against me. I am blessed with resiliency, tenacity, strong will and a single-mindedness and determination to overcome all my negative childhood circumstances.

My childhood was spent in the home of an alcoholic mom who tortured and abused me. We were dirt poor and lived in segregated Greenville, Mississippi. The whites lived on one side of the tracks and the blacks lived on the other side. I was repeatedly told I was not supposed to survive. Mom said, "You ain't nothing and you will never amount to anything" Faye, you ain't got it in you to survive." The community of Lick Skillet was filled with many people who had lost hope and were just waiting to die. Some killed themselves through suicide. Others destroyed themselves more slowly with alcohol and drugs, but later died a slow and painful death. The people never seemed happy. Lick Skillet was filled with hopeless and self-destructive people. Destruction surrounded me; mom and the neighbor's sought out something to help them to feel better. Most chose alcohol and drugs to help them escape our impoverished, segregated and hopeless circumstances. Day after day, I saw many negative and destructive individuals. They practiced behaviors that led to detrimental circumstances and permanent dire consequences. I witnessed husbands beat their wives, wives cheat on their husbands and husbands attack other men for cheating with their wives. Because the odds were stacked against me in my home, neighborhood and community, I desired a better life. I wanted a life that would be filled with hope and joy that I could share with many others. I learned the bible verse, "So a man think in his heart so is he". So if I wanted better it must start with my positive attitude and thinking. I never thought I was better than mom and the people in my neighborhood, but I always worked very hard at being better and different. As a child and adult I maintained a steadfast hope in God that He would make my life better and carry me to a better place. My hope has always been enough to pull me through and prevent me from many dark and terrible places. The more I write the more I understand why mom was so sick and unstable. As a child she was very angry, bitter, depressed and sad. She was very ill-equipped for all that life brought her way. My keen observation skills came directly from her. I learned from mom's torture and abuse the importance of always being prepared for any and everything that life brings my way. At the very least I am prepared to learn the lesson, so I would not repeat that mistake again. Without any effort at all she taught me how to be resilient, tenacious, determined and to have the power of not giving up, no matter what happens. She pushed me so hard, that she forced me to acquire many skill sets, but one set was the ability successfully survive her abuse and many other horrible events that came into my life. She did not possess any of these qualities; however she helped me to learn each one. Lick Skillet was a community filled with poor people who did not appear to have any hope for the future; therefore they gave up on life, which left failure their only option. Despite having the odds stacked against me, my hope and faith in God drove me to survive an abusive mother, in an unloving

17

home, careless neighborhood, and destructive community. God had greater work for me to do, so giving up was not an option. I never gave up no matter how uneven the playing field. As a tortured and abused child I wished for a book from an author who was willing to share his or her story of successfully surviving abuse at the hand of their parent.

"I Beat the Odds" is a book of triumph that offers hope to lift the broken spirits. The broken are searching for encouragement after they were tortured, abused and oppressed. This book will give joy to some; enlighten many and provide options for others. If I can positively impact one victim and inform one victimizer, then this book has done what I intended it to do. To those who have and are experiencing terrible circumstances, you can not only survive, but thrive. "I Beat the Odds" is the successful story of overcoming many destructive odds and successfully surviving those odds. Beating the Odds teaches its readers how to have a victorious life, on the other side of their pain. My prayer is that my story of triumph in the face of torture, abuse and violence will bring hope, joy, comfort and peace. I Beat the Odds is a resource to anyone who is feeling pain and sadness as a result of a difficult past or present circumstances.

I do not have a single memory of mom laughing, being sober or enjoying herself. She was either drunk or high, coming off being drunk or high or seeking to get drunk or high. She never seemed happy; which was evident by the fact that she drunk and cried 95% of the time, the other 5% she was sleeping. In spite of her cruelty to me, I loved her a great deal. I know I pitied her and wanted to help her. I was a young child who was also ill-equipped for all life brought to me, but I learned to swim upstream real fast. Each day she could not see beyond her next drink of alcohol; she could only see her pain which was self-inflicted. Every day she told me how much of a burden I was and how much she hated being my mother. She told me, "I hate my children, because y'all stole my youth from me. I never wanted to have any children. I just was having sex to get money." Day after day, I hated hearing her tell me this. I thought within myself, "I never asked to be born, so it was not my fault". She constantly blamed her ten children for her unhappiness. She believed or convinced herself, that if she would not have had ten children, her life would have been much happier. I used to think, "Well mom you should have thought about that ten children ago". She was always miserable. Misery was one her closest friends that she freely passed on to her kids as well as to every life she touched. She taught me as I observed her, the power of influence. She

20

showed me that "influence is power and power is influence". She had power over her ten children and she influenced each one of us.

She was married and divorced by age fourteen; had her first child at age sixteen; by the time she was thirty two she was the separated mother of ten children (eight males and two females). She spent her life in an alcohol and drug induced fog, where she tortured and blamed others for every negative and bad decision in her life. Some family legacies are a monetary inheritance, but mom's legacy was a destructive pattern of abuse, alcohol and drug addiction, blame-shifting, misery and bitterness. In spite of her family legacy, I learned to be responsible, accountable, committed and to love others and myself. However, I am still working through the negative family legacy she left for me.

Mom's School of Life

Some of my greatest life's lessons I gained by observing mom's school of life. Growing up living with an explosive alcohol and drug addicted mother was worse than watching a very bad train wreck in slow motion. She left me with two options; repeat the family legacy or change the family legacy. I guess it could have been more options, but those were the only two for me. Each victim and survivor has the same two options, plus the opportunity become a successful survivor. Repeating my family legacy is as simple as, 'abuse my children like mom abused me'. Changing the family legacy is my challenge. I took on this challenge, but I did not know that it required hard work daily. I changed and broke behaviors such as patterns of sexual and physical abuse, violence, and alcohol and drug addiction.

She was the worst yet most influential teacher of my life. As a result of her influence and impact I became a student and teacher of life. I am a student, because I was willing to submit my will under her authority and power. As I submitted I learned so much from her, that later helped me to successfully survive. I could have rebelled or been defiant; but I obeyed God by honoring and respecting her. I listened and paid attention to her and worked as hard as I could to turn all her negatives into positives for myself. Mom's school of life was my most intense classroom. I am a teacher, because I learned everything I could; I equipped myself and now I am equipping other victims how to successfully survive. In spite of all her flaws, she indirectly educated, equipped and prepared me very well. Today I know, mom meant it for my evil, but God meant it for my good. I beat the odds even though she meant them for my destruction, but

God turned it all for my good. It has been a long journey, but today I am thankful to God that she was my mom. I am also thankful for every negative word and event, because it brought me to this place and time in my life. I am a successful survival only because I understand that **success is not an event but a process over time**. It took me a lot of hard work and diligent lessons, but I finally arrived at a place where I can truly appreciate mom and the role she played in my life.

The bridge

Every bridge builder deserves a degree of respect for his or her labor. Mom, I respect because she labored to bring me here and God used her as the bridge to bring me where I am today. She was also a bridge builder, because without trying she taught me countless lessons. Lessons such as - it is up to me what I get out of every (negative or positive) situation and experience of my life. My life is filled with countless negative experiences, but true growth came when I stood back from each experience and committed to getting the most out each negative situation. I learned the full impact of torture, abuse, self-pity, and sadness. Her life was a testament to the dangers that result from not addressing unresolved issues. She taught me that your life is filled with much more quality and much more significance if you go through the process of healing. She showed me that any self-destructive behaviors can destroy me, my family, my neighborhood, community and world, if I do not address them. I am a successful survivor who knows that disaster is guaranteed, if I did not change my family legacy or break these self-destructive family patterns

I believe the reason mom turned to alcohol initially was to feel better and as a way to socially deal with others. Unfortunately, she grew dependent on alcohol and drugs and her addictions took her to dark, dark places, that she could never find her way back from. The journey of alcoholism and drug addiction took her farther than she wanted to go and it kept her much longer than she wanted to stay. She spent sixty one years in a fog of addiction, because she never figured out how to forgive, let go of the past and face her demons head-on. She did not know how to effectively deal with her pain. She lacked the courage and she allowed her pain, along with alcohol and prescription medication to destroy her family and her life.

Her addiction robbed my family in a few short years. I watched mom transition from a young, beautiful, vibrant and healthy lady into a self-destructive and bitter monster. Like a destructive tornado; she destroyed everyone and everything in her path. She treated alcohol and drugs like they were her best friends; never realizing they were actually her worst enemy. In the beginning, she believed that alcohol would ease her pain. It was clear that her addictions were destroying family; either she did not realize it or she did not care. She believed that alcohol and drugs temporarily transported her to a different place. They were a comforters and friends. The brief peace she hoped she would have with alcohol soon became her worst nightmare. Quickly her new comforter turned against us; she became an abuser and violator of her children. Whether intoxicated or sober, she was plagued by unaddressed mental illness and carried the weight of the world on her shoulders. She was always depressed, unstable and disconnected. Addiction magnified her personality; it made her more explosive, volatile and abusive. Her addiction did not make her reclusive, it just magnified her reclusiveness. She sat alone intoxicated for days with her head hung down, hand over her mouth and talking to herself. She was filled with great pride and self-pity which prevented her from reaching out for help. She often said, "I have a house full of kids and we were poor, hungry and struggling, people never offered to help me." I know we received help, it may not have been the help she wanted, but I know certain people helped. Ms. Pearl Duncan quietly and discretely handed us cooked food over the fence. Ms. Rosie gave us fruit cakes every Christmas. Other neighbors gave us clothes for me to wear. Mother Rose was a mentor, counselor and mid-wife who delivered some of my siblings. She gave money, food and basically adopted JD and I. In spite of all she received, she chose to focus on what she did not receive. **This taught me that it was my choice whether I took the negative or positives from each situation in life.** Mom had the "gift for focus". But she chose to focus on the negatives not the positives and on destructive not constructive. Right now I can visualize her sitting there in the kitchen, in a chair, with a glass of alcohol and a cigarette in one hand, with her other hand covering her face. She sat in the kitchen for days at a time, with her body slumped over and her head hung low to the ground, as she cried in agony. What could I possibly take from a woman who spent days at a time intoxicated and isolated? I learned determination; commit to something and stick to it until it is totally complete. She helped me realize that I could do anything I want to do, if I want it bad enough. She was filled with self-pity; which meant she was always the victim in every story she told. My childhood was sad for two reasons; one because I could not help her to come out of her darkness and move to a better place. Secondly she treated me like she hated me. My helplessness is why I am a motivator; I could not help her or myself. I am committed to helping people fight against darkness and help them avoid that same darkness that mom got lost in.

Mom was overcome by her destructive family legacy; her personal battle with addiction, poverty, a host of destructive family problems, and racism living in Greenville, Mississippi. By God's grace, I beat these odds. Our first house was a two room small red tool shed that had been poorly converted into a small family house. It was located in the poorest part of Greenville on the south end of town. I lived in constant terror even before mom started torturing me. The red tool shed had snakes in the walls and floors. This was just another reminder of our desperate living conditions. I did not care that we were very poor, nor did I care that we did not possess many of life's necessities. But I did care about my relationship with my mother. The greatest impact on my child and adulthood was being tortured and abused by mom. She was very ashamed of our poverty; she was paranoid and spent a great deal of time believing that everyone in our poor community was rich. She said, "They are richer than me and they spend most of their time looking down on me and talking about me and making fun of me."

Lick Skillet was filled with very poor people, but they managed to have money for their pleasures. There were gamblers on every street corner shooting dice, hustlers, pimps, prostitutes, child molesters, cafés and small party clubs. Homemade liquor houses that sold corn liquor to kids and adults. There were four corner grocery stores, and hundreds of families that lived in shacks and shot-gun houses. Everyone was very poor from what I could see; yet mom convinced herself that she was the most unfortunate person in our poor neighborhood. Most of the poor people in our community were like crabs in a bucket. They did everything they could to prevent one another from rising above their circumstances and succeeding. She treated me worse than she treated our neighbor; because she felt we were her enemy. She would say, "I can never have anything because y'all kids take everything that I have. I hate having kids. If I didn't have all y'all kids, I could get a decent man." She convinced herself that we were out to get her, which explains why she abused me. Since she saw me as her enemy, by hurting me, she was protecting herself from me, her enemy. Most of her time was spent intoxicated and isolated in the kitchen sitting alone in misery. While isolated she constantly complained about how bad life had been to her. She cried about how people hated her and how much she despised those same people.

But when she did not have any money and needed a fix, she went to those same hateful neighbors, pretended to like them until she was intoxicated. As soon as she was intoxicated, she cursed them out and told them that she hated them. She would say, "Faye if you see a fool bump his head, before he use you". She trusted no one and believed that everyone was out to get her. She said, "Faye, you must get them before they get you". Whenever she saw me being kind to people she would say, "Faye, you are such a fool for being nice to that person". If I was polite to a male she would say, "You must be sleeping with him". But she would not say, "sleep with", she was much more profane. She was a very beautiful woman and she was well aware of her beauty. She would say, "Watch how they whistle when I pass by and watch how many heads I turn when I pass by these men." She was an expert at manipulating anyone, especially men. She was not afraid to use anyone, at any time and for any reason. She was a master at taking advantage of people; the people had no idea that they were being taken by her. There was no shortage of men in her life. During the early years, she loved her men almost as much as she loved her liquor. She had her selection of any man she wanted, but she liked the ones she could most easily manipulate, because she did not want to work real hard to get what she wanted. One of her many male friends once defended me, but he soon lived to regret it. His name was John Henry. He had dated mom for several months and silently watched her abuse and mistreat me. John Henry said, "Celeste, why do you treat Faye so bad? She is a beautiful, smart and respectful child." Mom said, "Why do you care, you must want to sleep with her. Are you here for her or me? Get out of my house." He shut-up and never said anything else again. She used her beauty and her charm to get exactly what she wanted, whenever she wanted it. John Henry soon found out that he was just one of the rustlers, because she had her pick up the liter. What she wanted more than any man was to be intoxicated and high. She said, "Faye, John Henry want you not me, but the only reason I keep you around is for you to serve me." She was so paranoid that she made it impossible for any person to be around her. She saw ghost where they did not exist and monster where there were no monsters. After growing up under her instruction, it was very difficult not to be like her; she was a malicious, empty, vain and cruel person.

Chapter II - The Kitchen

Between the ages three to five in the evenings when she was not working, she would say, "Faye come walk up the streets with me". "Walk up the streets" meant it was time for her to go to her friend Ms. Bernice house. Ms. Bernice made and sold 'corn liquor' and drank out of her house. She supplied mom with alcohol to drink whenever mom wanted it. I spent countless hours with mom at Ms. Bernice house sitting on her front porch. I listened to her and mom talk about hard times and the neighborhood people. Ms. Bernice was a moonshiner like my Aunt Darling. Ms. Bernice lived on Hinds street which was down the street and around the corner from our home on Short Clay Street.

I never liked Hinds street because it was filled with unsavory people. In route to Ms. Bernice house we had to pass Joe Long corner store, where there were men standing, sitting, leaning and bending over the side walk gambling with dice. There was never any walking room on the corner of Short Clay and Hinds streets, because the gamblers were always in the way gambling. They were all adult males who were perverted and loved saying and trying to do inappropriate things to us young girls as we passed by. Joe Long corner store was located on the corner of Short Clay Street and Hinds Street. When mom drank she also had to smoke cigarettes; when she ran out of them, it was my job to go to Joe Long store and buy her some cigarettes. I went to Joe Long's store to get mom's cigarettes and Joe Long was inside waiting on customers to come inside. Joe Long was a child molester who owned a corner store. Every time I went into his store to purchase mom cigarettes he would offer me free candy or cookies, in exchange for sex with him. As hungry as I was, I still refused. I hated to go to his store and I hated the things he said to me even more.

Lick Skillet was filled with poor people who were mostly trying to find some hope, while making an honest living in order provide for their families. But the portion of Hinds streets, at least the portion that we lived on, was the worst part of Hinds Street. I never felt safe walking along Hinds Street, especially when I had to go into Joe Long corner store. One day mom said, "Faye lets walk up the street", as we approached the corner of Short Clay and Hinds street, I heard several loud gunshot blast. Mom and I quickly turned and went back home. Later that day we found out that one man shot and killed another man in the house next door to Joe Long corner store. Shortly after this incident, Ms. Bernice died and mom was devastated. These two events triggered a drastic change in mom's social identity, so she stop going,

'up the streets.'

After mom stopped going "up the street", she spent

the majority of her time in isolation. After a long day

of working in the cotton field she would go to the

corner store to purchase her supplies. She

purchased some chopped ham, bread, Kool-Aid,

Juicy Fruit chewing gum, alcohol and cigarettes. She

returned home, gave us the food, took the rest and

put her alcohol in the refrigerator. Before she put her

alcohol away; she poured herself a glass of alcohol, lit

a cigarette and went directly to the outside of our

house. She spent the rest of the night isolated sitting

outside drinking alcohol and smoking cigarettes. I

noticed she had started holding long conversations

with someone I could not see.

As young as I was, I watched her alcohol consumption increased and isolation consumed her. This led to depression and sadness taking over. Before I realized it she moved from outside and into the kitchen isolation. While in kitchen isolation a great darkness took over and consumed her; she refused to be disturbed, which resulted in her torturing and abusing me. In the beginning she only spent days in the kitchen, drinking and talking to her invisible friends. The kitchen was her drinking and isolation sanctuary. I knew she wanted to leave us, but she had also lost the ability and desire to maneuver through life on her own. So she stayed home, but I paid the highest price for her decision to stay. She made life miserable for me and punished me every day of her life. She told me that I reminded her of what she could have become, but because she had so many children, she did not have the courage to move forward.

She said, "Faye, I hate you because you are coming and I am going. You are young and I am old." Through her alcoholism and reclusiveness she decided that she hated parenting and did not want to be saddled with ten children. Some parents have the courage to leave their kids, so they won't do great harm to them. But mom figured out a different way to leave and disconnect; she disconnected mentally and emotionally without physically leaving. She did more damage by staying home than she would have had she left. She told me "You ought to be happy that I stayed, because a lot of mammies would have left a house full of children". I believe she found the kitchen safe and secure, which is why she went there. It seemed clear to me that she was a recluse, who wanted to be left alone. Unfortunately she had ten children and we lived in a very small one bedroom "shotgun" house. Since she did not want to be bothered, isolation was the option that she chose. Her desire to leave was overpowered by fear of what the neighbors would say if she left us; so she stayed and tortured me every day she was alive. She left us; but she did not physically move one inch. She said, "Faye, you are not just a problem, but a burden to me. Why don't you go find some man to marry, so he can take you off my hands"?

Even though she was in the home with us, there were three times I was guaranteed to see her. First, I saw her when she was going to the bathroom; second when she was giving me orders and third during the hours of abuse. She was physically in the house, but she had been emotionally gone for years. Her emotional disconnection from me, made it easy for her to abuse me. She absolutely hated being home with us. She proudly told me, "I hate you kids and I wish I was somewhere else, anywhere but here with you kids." Even though she was at home; I missed her my entire childhood. As young as I was, I tried the best way I knew to spend as much quality time around her. She had the most beautiful silky and curly hair, but she hated her hair. When she allowed me to I washed, oiled, combed, brushed and hot combed her hair. But I had limited access to her, because her moods swung from cold to hot in a split second. One moment the house would be quiet and the next second a hurricane called Celeste stormed through our house destroying everything and everyone in her path.

I remember standing in the kitchen door saying, "Hey mom can I come in?' She would say, "Hell no, you black whore, just leave me the hell alone." She did not see the need for bonding with me. She preferred alcoholism and reclusiveness over her kids and family bonding. She said, "I have lots of regrets about being tied down with such a great burden as ten children." Every day she drank more, sinking further into the abyss of addiction and depression. The collection of depression, drinking and isolation brought more days and nights of torture and abuse for me. As a child I had a sense that she was devastated and overwhelmed by her circumstances, but what could I do? I noticed that she did not take care of herself. She never bathed, showered or washed up. She sat in the kitchen for weeks at a time. I knew she was clearly drowning. I often told her that she was beautiful and how much I loved her. I spent lots of energy trying to make her feel better. As I said before, I did small loving gestures such as wash, oil, and hot comb her hair. I tried to get her to bath, but she was too consumed by addiction and depression.

I did anything I could think of to let her know she was loved. I would have done almost anything to save her, spend time with her and to be close to her. I was a very sensitive kid and I could see she was in trouble. Honestly watching her drown was more devastating than experiencing her abuse. Being a kid, I was absolutely helpless. The emotions of helplessness still swell up in me today, just like they did then.

Destructive family legacy; alcoholism; depression; reclusiveness; shame and guilt; single parenting of ten children; being dirt poor and couldn't feed those ten children; no real family connections or support; racism in Mississippi and societal pressures were just too much for her. These pressures and many others destroyed her. I know she didn't have the intestinal fortitude and strength to successfully survive the pressures life brought to her. Since she was so self-destructive; she forced me to become determined to become a successful survivor. It seemed like it happened overnight, but it was over the process of time. I knew she was drowning, but I did not know how to help her to hold her up to breathe and swim. The truth was as devastating as things were she did not want to be saved. She would often beg, "God please come and get me. I hate living and I want to die". She was the first person to teach me, "If someone does not want to be saved, than you cannot save them, no matter how hard you try". In spite of all her weaknesses, in her own mixed up way, she was a very proud, but stubborn woman. Her pride would not allow her to ask for help or admit she was an alcoholic. She was too afraid to admit that her family legacy and alcoholism was destroying her and her family. By 1971, we had moved from the rear in the little red shed, to the front of Short Clay Street to a very small house called a 'shot-gun house". It was bigger than the shed, but it was still not big enough to properly fit ten people. Unless you grew up in a shed or shot-gun house, you can only imagine how small this limited space really was. Try to imagine it, seven males, two females and one adult all in a one bedroom shot-gun house?

I have three children and I have felt overwhelmed; but she had ten mouths to feed. I cannot imagine what she was feeling on the inside. Her feeling of being overcrowded and pushed out is probably what magnified her need for isolation. Her desperate need for isolation and peace turned into a nightmare for the rest of us. She would say, "All I want is some peace, y'all kids are driving me crazy. Go away from me, go outside. Do whatever you want, just get away from me". Looking back I can see her desperate need for space and her cry out for help. Unfortunately, she did not have the strength to reach out for help, but she internalized her pain. Later her unaddressed pain triggered her inner monster, which destroyed her family.

In 1975 my older brother JD joined the United States Army. This should have been the beginning of major economic growth for our family. JD left home and sent a two hundred dollar monthly allotment check back to the family. This was huge, considering up until his departure we had survived on a one hundred twenty dollar monthly welfare check and four hundred fifty dollars in food stamps, which is what Mississippi gave to a single mother with nine kids. This financial increase should have been the start of wonderful changes since she constantly complained about being poor and never having money. But as soon as God blessed our finances to increase, she could not handle the sudden monetary increase. She sank even deeper into sadness and depression; she drank more and isolated even more, which resulted in more abuse against me. JD sent a two hundred monthly allotment home, but mom's drinking was completely out-of-control, so the two hundred dollars went directly to feeding her addictions. Instead of mom using the money wisely, she created new problems for herself and for our family. She repeatedly demanded to be left alone; she practically lived in the kitchen isolated until the hours of abuse. Every day I was told, "I hate being your mom and I would rather be doing anything else, but parenting you." Listening and receiving her words was hard, but watching her self-destruct was even harder. She said, "The reason I went to the cotton-field was to escape being at home with you kids. I never wanted to have any girls."

My older brothers were just as unhealthy and destructive as our family legacy. They saw how self-destructive she had become, but because they did not want to deal with her addiction, they simply sent an allotment check home every month. Instead of helping the family by addressing mom's addiction and to ease their guilt, they all sent a check each month. In 1976 my brother Larry also joined the Army and sent two hundred dollars. In 1978 my brother Carl joined the Army and sent one hundred fifty dollars; and in 1980, Danny joined the Army and sent two hundred dollars. So by 1981 our economic outlook should have improved tremendously, but we never saw a penny of that money. Her addictions consumed it; what she did not spend feeding her addictions, the corner store owners cheated her out of it. She had several corner store accounts where she bought alcohol and cigarettes. She also had corn liquor accounts that she used all through the month, but paid each one at the beginning of each month.

Corner store owners and corn liquor sellers were taking most of her money and providing her with alcohol and cigarettes through the entire month.

She stayed home and spent all of her time in the kitchen drinking, isolating and wallowing in self-pity and misery. She had lost her way through the fog of alcoholism. She spent most of her time mixing addiction and religion; confusing her practice of addiction and religion with a false sense of spiritual security. She was totally consumed with dying, so she spent all her isolated time begging God to let her die. Since she spent most of her time in the kitchen; she almost burned the house down many times, because she would drink and try to cook at 2 and 3am. Many mornings I was disturbed out my sleep coughing and smelling food burning on the stove. I got up to find her slumped over her chair, drunk out of her mind, asleep or just sitting in the kitchen in a daze. The kitchen was her sanctuary and a close distance to her liquor and the gas stove to light her cigarettes.

Every word and behavior mom displayed told me that she did not need me. But the problem was this was a false sense of security, because she could not have survived without me. She was totally reclusive and never left the house. She sent me to handle every financial transaction she needed to be handled. She protected "her food" from us; she would yell, scream and curse at us if she thought we were trying to enter her sanctuary. Because her emotions ran from 0 to 200 in a split second, I learned to ask questions to test for safety of entering her sanctuary. I would ask, "Mom can I come into the kitchen", some days she would say, "Come on in, Faye". But most days she was in her place of mental torture. So she would say, "Hell nall, get away from me". So whatever she said is what I did. I guess from time to time guilt would visit her in the kitchen and she would yell out to us, "At least I am at home with you no good brats. I could have been like one of those mammies that put a pillow over your head and smothered you, but I did not". These words made me sick to my stomach and I could not grasp how she felt proud of herself. If I dared to enter the kitchen without her giving me permission to enter while she was intoxicated she would yell and curse, "You black whore, you ain't worth the sex it took to get you here, get out of here". Other times she would say, "You just dumb and stupid get out of here". It was clear as crystal to me that mom was dangerous, but what that meant I was not sure about. All my life I have struggled with the knowledge and acceptance that because she hated herself, she did not possess the capacity to love me or anyone else. In theory that sounds reasonable, but

53

how do I accept this and how do I live with a person who hates themselves. Knowledge is power; but I did not feel powerful because I had the knowledge that she did not love me.

On some occasions, she would isolate to the kitchen and drink (binging) for several weeks without any sleep. I would ease up to the kitchen entry-way and listen to her as she had full conversations with herself and with her invisible friends. During these times I don't think she was aware of what she was doing or how it impacted us. The conversation was just as lively as if she was having a conversation with another person. She was in the kitchen alone, but she was giving information, asking questions and answering questions just like it was another person in the kitchen with her. As a young kid her behavior absolutely terrified me.

As a kid I did not know anything about mental illness, but I did know mom and everyone in her family were "OUT OF THEIR MIND." I just believed that their minds were not screwed on tight or at the least, they were missing something in their brains. As mom talked to these invisible people she would say, "I don't know", "He is crazy", "I don't know who he think I am". She never had a clue that I was at the entry-way listening to her. The thing I realized from listening to her was she was angry most of the time, even when she was alone.

Mom talking to invisible people was not the worst thing that terrified me as she isolated in that kitchen. What I learned about mom was just when I thought I had seen the worst part of her, I had only scratched the surface. One of those days occurred one summer day after I came home from playing basketball. She was sitting alone in the kitchen as usual talking erratically, rambling and intoxicated out of her mind. I

went to the kitchen entry-way to check in on her. I

noticed that her arms were hanging down at her side

with blood running from the middle to the bottom of

her arm. I was terrified, but I did not know what to do.

She had been on one of her binges where she had

been drinking for weeks on end without any sleep.

She felt bugs crawling all over her, so she was trying

to remove them. She had a safety pin stuck inside

her arm with her veins and arteries hooked

underneath the metal safety pin. This scared me so

bad; I asked her, "Mom what are you doing"? She

said, "Faye they are crawling all over me, they are

crawling all over me". The blood was streaming down

her arms, but she did not indicate that she felt any

pain; she was more focused on the bugs she believed

were crawling all over her body. I did not see any

bugs, not one crawling on her. She made such a

strong case I thought I must be missing the bugs, so I looked even closer but I did not see them. I asked again, "Why are you using a safety pin to pull your veins and arteries out of your arm?" She said, "Faye they are crawling on me, don't you see them; they are crawling all over me". She continued to scratch herself, while pulling at the safety pin. She repeatedly told me how much they were crawling all over her. This became part of what she did every day and it terrified me. She spent hours upon hours using safety pins to pull her veins and arties out until open sores formed on her arms, legs and scratch marks covered her body.

One day, when I arrived in the house I was hungry from playing basketball and wanted something to eat. However, I saw mom in such trauma and distress, I forgot all about my hunger and concentrated more on how to help her. As I watched mom I realized how much I loved her, how much I wanted to make it better for her and how much I pitied her. I realized how helpless she was and when she refused to go to the hospital, I knew how helpless I really was.

I knew she was dangerous, because her behavior was unstable, strange, bizarre and insane. One moment we were in bed sound asleep and the next minute I felt hot water fly through the window fan. So many nights, it is 3am, she would boil pots of hot water go outside to my bedroom window and throw the hot water through the fan. This was her attempt to burn me out of the bedroom. I was the victim and she was the victimizer. It did not matter to me what she did, she was mom and I loved her a great deal. As a misguided kid I felt my job was to make her better and protect her. Whenever she would allow me, I cleaned her up, I put her to bed and I excused her mean and cruel words and told myself "She is just drunk". While I was helping her to bed, she said, "Faye, you are black, fat, ugly and no man will ever want you". She was and still is the cruelest person I have ever encountered. Because she was so cruel, we learned to sneak in the kitchen when she went to the bathroom and get us some quick and instant food to eat. I remember thinking, "Why does she hate me so much"? She did not eat much food, but she ate a lot of sweets which curbed her appetite. But she always had an appetite for drinking alcohol, fussing and cursing. I used to wonder, "Why did God put me in this family"?

Not only did she drink in the kitchen, but any and all transactions took place in the kitchen. She did not leave the house anymore, she sent me to the corner store with a grocery list which included alcohol and cigarettes. She instructed me to get the house bills together, bring them to her in the kitchen, she gave me the money to pay them, but she never left the kitchen. She did not have any friends; she isolated herself from any friend's she previously had.

Eating Disorder

As a result of childhood food deprivation I developed an eating disorder. Every penny I got as a child I went to the corner store and bought something sweet to eat, because the sweets curved my appetite. At 8 years old, I was sneaking and cooking the family dinners and all the holiday meals. Mom's addictions made her uninterested and incapable of taking care of self or the family. As a matter of fact, if she did not have children she would have drunk herself to death much earlier. I was a fighter who survived and I became a soldier, which makes me a leader. My childhood abuse cultivated my leadership capabilities. I was very mature and responsible; I took care of my mom and two younger siblings. I was given too much responsibility too fast, so I lost myself in the process. I know I was so busy caring for mom and everyone else that I did not know how to take care of myself. I was filled with such ambivalence, I loved her, but I also hated her. I felt obligated to her, but I was so angry that she did not care enough to take care of me. I was mad because I never felt loved by her. Whenever I was around her I felt hatred from her. She said, "Faye I hate you. I did not want you. You are just a link in my chain." I felt like a stranger in my childhood own home. She did not take any interest in me or how much I hurt. She did not care about how isolated I was from my friends and family. I did not have friends who understood my pain, because I was too ashamed to share my hurt outside of my home. She would say, "Faye, why would anyone ever love you, you ain't worth loving. I hate you and they will hate you too." Because I experienced so much rejection, abuse and abandonment from mom, I did not believe anyone could ever really love me or that I was worthy of anyone loving me. I told myself, "if the greatest love of all is that of a mother and my mother hated me, then who else would ever love me". She crippled me emotionally which made me a mess for future relationships. Isolated and alone, I did not have anyone to express my hurt and emotional pain to, so I ate myself through my pain and suppressed everything. I spent my entire childhood searching and hoping for safety and love. Since torture and abuse is all I have known since childhood, real love had escaped me until I had children of my own. It is important for me to tell my story, because most people can't imagine that a mother could hate her children.

Chapter III – My Smile

"I hate your smile, your gap-teeth, your black face and I hate your white teeth. Yuck you make me sick". Some parents greet their child with a friendly smile; others greet them with a hug and kiss. But my mom greeted me every day by telling me how much she hated my smile; she hated me and hated everything about me. My smile threatened her in ways that I still don't understand. I did not have control over my situation, but I did have control over my smile. My smile was my weapon I used to fight mom. Since my smile bothered her so much, I smiled even more. I controlled my smile and I determined how much of my pain she was going to have access to. Through my smile I controlled the level of pain I was going to allow her to know about. She beat and beat me, but I did not cry. I smiled, because I knew early on that she was so miserable that she wanted me and everyone around her to be miserable. But I understood that I needed to appear happy in front of her, because that was the only power I had. When I was younger, I cried in front of her and she would say, "Faye, you are so weak, I hate weak people and I hate you." **My tears gave her power and control over me.** So I refused to let her see me cry anymore; to protect my heart from her, I smiled all the time. I knew she wanted to break my spirit, but my smile made her think that she was not penetrating to my spirit. **My smile made her very, very, very angry, but it gave me power over her.** She was a diseased addict who took pleasure in destroying the spirits of her children and others.

I grew up in a society and culture that taught me to honor, respect and obey my parents. My society also said a parent was supposed to love their children.

But where was society when I was tortured, abused and mistreated every day of my childhood?

Therefore, I wore a mask called my smile; in order to protect my heart and myself from the monster called mom. I could never let her know how much she hurt me, so I always looked at her and smiled through my pain. She would say, "I hate everything about you. What are you smiling about?" I learned in childhood the importance of daily renewing my decision not to give up. I have decided that I was a successful survivor because I did not allow her to break my spirit which is why I beat the odds. These odds included a mother who was an explosive, volatile addict who took great pleasure in torturing me. My smile helped me to get through so many days and nights of torture and abuse. It has become extremely important each day for me to motivate myself, my children and every life I encounter. I focus on God, while realizing what

He has delivered me from all the odds that was stacked against me. Through my smile I have taught and reassured myself, my children and countless others to give our very best to every task that our hands and hearts touch. Even though I grew up feeling unloved, unwanted and sad; I learned the power and influence of a positive smile. As a child, I figured out that true contentment, power, discipline and control starts within me (inside) and goes without (outside to others). I knew mom wanted to break me, but I knew if I smiled she could not determine whether or not she was breaking my spirit. My smile was not only a mask with mom, but the world; so that people would not know how worthless I truly felt inside.

Since childhood I have been very disappointed with people; I still find it difficult to trust them. My childhood was filled with people who heard and saw my abuse, but did not move to action to help me. My smile was the mask that made everything look and seem like it was ok, because that is what made people more comfortable. Some people want to feel comfortable, even if it is at the expense of an abused child. I wore my mask and pretended it was all wonderful, but I was slowly dying on the inside. Mom, my family, my older brothers, neighbors, the police and the Department of Human Services all saw first-hand my abuse, but none of them helped me. They all knew, heard and saw my pain, but did nothing to help. Since they really did not care, why did they deserve the privilege of seeing my real pain? So I put a permanent mask on my face to hide my true pain, to protect myself, but also protect them.

My smile put people at ease, even if I was experiencing turmoil on the inside. As a young child I noticed that the kids that were sad and depressed got ignored and overlooked by adults and made fun of by other kids. The adults in my community refused to deal with me unless I was smiling and appearing happy. As an adult I find that people still need me to smile, in order to deal with me. Adults gravitate to the smiling and happy child, not to the sad and depressed child. I also noticed that people like to be comfortable not uncomfortable. Sad and depressed kids make adults very uncomfortable, so they get ignored and not dealt with properly. Most people do everything they can to keep their level of comfort. I learned that it took much more work to deal with the sad and depressed kid, than to deal with the smiling and happy kid. My book is meant to reach that sad and depressed kid as well as that happy kid. Smiling through my pain and appearing to have it together took on a life of its own. My smile put people at ease and it helped them to feel like they really knew me and what was going on inside my head. My smiled made people feel whatever they needed to feel.

Sometimes people don't help for a host of reasons, but one of the reason people don't help is because they just don't care enough to help. They see the abuse, care in the moment that it is happening, but after they pass that moment, they don't care anymore, so they move forward and forget what they just saw. I encourage you to move into action the very moment that you understand that abuse exist. My smile masked and covered so much worthlessness, self-doubt and lack of motivation for me. For thirty two years I wore a mask in front of mom. I bought into her abused, believed what she said and I felt worthless as a result. Early on I had to teach myself how to smile and love myself or appear to love myself; because mom taught me self-hatred, worthlessness and self-doubt. I learned early as a young child that no one enjoyed being around a sad and depressed person. I wanted to appear to have it together and I did not want them to see my real pain. So I created a mask, a cover which is my smile.

I am extrovert, but mom was an introvert. Extroversion is one of my God-given gifts. People were drawn to me and I was drawn to them. I was warm, open, outgoing, pleasant, friendly and loving. She was shallow, cold, closed, introverted, mean, unfriendly and unloving. We were mother and daughter, but we were as different as day and night. She hated me for being what she was not. She tortured and abused me because she was determined to break my spirit and beat those great qualities out of me. She saw my smile as my greatest quality, which is why she did all she could to destroy my smile. I possessed the God-given talent to captivate the attention of others just by my smile and personality.

Mom was a very beautiful woman, but very insecure, introverted, awkward and shy. I was never afraid of talking to anyone at any time, about anything. But mom despised me for possessing these qualities. She would say, "I hate you, you talk too much and you embarrass me, everyday".

When I was very young, she took me everywhere with her, because she was very uncomfortable with people. I later realized it was only because of her self-doubt, shyness and self-hatred that she took me with her. Because she was uncomfortable passing the neighbors houses alone, so I was kind of a buffer for her. She would say, "Faye come walk up the streets to Bernice house". I was very excited to go anywhere with my mom, because I adored her, in spite of all her flaws. The problem was we had to pass several neighbors houses to get to Ms. Bernice's house and mom did not like these particular neighbors. These women had affairs with her husband, JD. Sr. and she did not like them since the affair. Each time she passed their houses she was reminded of the affairs so she was very uncomfortable to pass by. As a child I did not know all this background information until once when we were passing by and I spoke to them, as I always did. As soon as we passed by them she said, "Faye, don't speak to those whores because they slept with my husband. I hate them and I hate you for speaking to them."

Because she hated them, she wasted a great deal of time drinking and cursing about those female neighbors. She would repeatedly say, "I can't stand those whores they screwed my husband". As we passed by their houses mom and I would speak to them. It never failed after she returned home she would attack me for speaking to those neighbors.

She would make fun of me and say, "You are such a fool for speaking to those whores". This was very confusing to me because we both spoke to them, but she would beat me for speaking for them. Mom would say, "You seemed so happy to speak to them". I could never figure out the madness that was going on inside of her. She was always so unhappy.

I always managed to smile and maintain an upbeat personality in front of mom, especially when she beat me. I never understood her mental instability; neither did I blame her for being unstable. I always hoped my love would be enough to pull her away from the dark place that she lived in, but I was wrong. My love for her was more than enough, but she did not want to receive love, she was stuck in misery. She was drowning in addiction, knew she was drowning and was satisfied in drowning. I often told her that she was drinking herself to death. She told me, "Faye, I hate your smile, your red lips, your white teeth and your black face". Because of her physical, mental, and verbal abuse, I never felt good about myself. Despite my inner turmoil, I planted a smile on my face and pretended that I was in a great place, but I never really felt good about myself, nor did I really love myself. I could never shake the sadness, self-hatred and depression that she passed on to me. No matter my pain, I always managed to smile and where my mask in front of others. I was determined to wear my mask on the outside even if I was miserable on the inside.

Despite living in a very small house with only one bedroom, we were not a close family unit. The closeness of any family has absolutely nothing to do with physical proximity. Mom was within hugging distance, but she never hugged me, not once during my entire childhood. She was within reaching distance, but she never reached outside of herself to address my needs. My brothers were going their own way, but I was left in the care of the monster, called mom. Mom was not the only one to make me feel unloved, my oldest brother JD, would tell people, "That is not my sister and I am ashamed of my family". Feeling love, nurtured, secure, safe and well balanced were emotions that I never experienced during childhood. The emotions I was most familiar with during childhood were disconnection, loneliness and emptiness. I knew my mom and my siblings were in the house with me, but I did not feel a real connection to any of them. I remember looking for positive television characters and their behavior to emulate and duplicate. I was surrounded by a mom, siblings, family, neighbors and a community that hated me, so I needed some hope and I needed someone to love me.

We had two aunts and other family in Greenville, Mississippi, but they were not connected to our family. The only time I saw my family was when they all got together for the "family gatherings" to drink, party and fight. Family gatherings always resulted in family disconnection for the next 6 months. The reason mom and her sisters were not close was because they spent too much time drinking, not forgiving each other and destroying one another. This family disconnection sent the message to me that your siblings and your family is not important. Mom and her sisters only had a relationship out of convenience.

Aunt Lillie, mom's oldest sister, was 27 years older and they had a love and hate relationship, they love to hate each other. Aunt Lillie was a mean and cold alcoholic, who isolated from her family. She had two passions; Old Charter whiskey and abusive men. Aunt Darling was 20 years older than mom, an alcoholic who made, drank and sold corn liquor. She supplied mom liquor and money whenever she wanted it. Mom and I would walk about two miles across town to Aunt Darling's house to borrow money and get corn liquor. Aunt Darling's house was a house of degradation; it was filled with drunks, prostitutes and criminals. My Aunts were very much like mom, they were not affectionate, but violent toward each other. Mom, my siblings, my aunts, and neighborhood, it was all negative and destructive. I was the first girl among seven brothers, but they treated me like they hated me and I did not matter very much. Due to my negative surroundings, I was desperately searching for positive people, places, and things. Television offered me an escape and positive alternatives to my negative home, family and surroundings. My favorite childhood shows were Little House on the Prairie, Bonanza, The Big Valley,

The Walton's, Good Times, Charlie's Angels, Fat Albert and anything with Bill Cosby. Because on these television shows through good, bad or ugly they loved, nurtured, supported, encouraged and were always there for each other. These shows gave me hope that family and friends could be sober, happy and loving, if they wanted it and were willing to work together.

I knew mom never loved me; but I smiled and wore my mask to hide all my pain. I always hoped that one day she would nurture, hug or give me any small display of affection that indicated that she cared. I was invisible and treated like I was worthless to mom and my family. I spent so many days wondering, "Why was I born?" As a kid I watched the movie "Lady Sings the Blues", because I connected emotionally with Billy Holiday's struggle with her addiction to alcohol. The music also resonated with me, the song, Good Morning Heartache" I totally related to that song. I watched that movie and listened to "Good morning Heartache" repeatedly. I understood first-hand brokenness, loneliness, emptiness, sadness and devastation. I knew I could help mom, if she allowed me to; because I was experiencing the same emotions she was experiencing. The lyric of the song resonated with me because I lived and felt every line. I remember thinking, "Mom doesn't love me, she beats me for no reason, she tells me she hates me, what am I to do with all of this pain". But the next morning I got up and put my mask on my face and went forward to face the world. My smile took on a life of its own. I was sad, but I could brighten other people's day and hopefully they would not feel as sad as I did. I remember disliking my smile because mom told me that she disliked it so much. I could not hit her, punish her or beat her like she was beating me. So I smiled because it was a form of power for me over her. Since she said she hated my smile so much, I smiled all the time in front of her just to make her mad. I remember thinking and feeling like I had absolutely no one to care for me, so I could not give all my power over to her, so I smiled and I smiled lot. My smile said to her, you can't break me.

Mom was terrible on every level possible; she was physically, mentally and psychologically abusive. She also refused to buy me any clothes to wear. I had seven older brothers, who passed their clothes from one brother to the next brother. But I was the first girl born after she had seven boys, so surely I was going to get some nice clothes. However, she did not buy me any girl clothing, she forced me to wear my brother's clothes. She did not buy me any undergarments, if I got bras or panties; they were her old ones that she could no longer wear. Her old

undergarments were worn, torn and too big, so I had

to put safety pins in them in order to wear them. So, I

could not and still don't understand for the life of me,

why she did this to me. I remember the

embarrassment I felt and experienced when the kids

at school talked about my brothers clothing and how I

dressed like a boy. I was so embarrassed and

ashamed, but I still smiled. My smile covered my

internal pain. The kids were very cruel and made fun

of me for wearing my brothers clothing. I had one pair

of girl pants; they were a pair of red and white

checker board pants, so I decided to wash and wear

them every day. The kids still made fun of me

because I wore one pair of pants; but to me, this was

better than being made fun of because I wore my

brother's clothes. I just felt very empty and sad

inside, but of course I had to hold all this inside

because if mom spotted any weakness in me, she would make fun of me for that weakness. The real reason I never wrote my story is because I did not possess the strength to re-open and re-live all of my old wounds. As I write I am being forced to honestly admit my pain, address it and slowly heal as I write. As I write about all the sadness each moment I am transported to the past to my childhood back in those small shacks in Greenville, Mississippi. I feel all the pain now that I felt then. It feels like a doctor is cutting my heart out of my chest, but I am awake experiencing all the pain. I see her face, I feel her cruelty and insensitivity; her goal was "to break my spirit". Maybe that was not her thought process, but that was the message that I received. I always gave love freely to others; because I grew up so unloved by mom. My torture, abuse and pain I have learned to accept and deal with, but it is hard to accept that she did not love me. Even as I write this book, I hear her voice in my head today just as clear as I heard it many years ago saying, "Faye you ain't nothing, you ain't never going to be nothing and I hate you. "I should have put a pillow on your head when you first got her and smothered your black ass".

How does a mother give birth to a child, keep that child and then spend the rest of her life torturing that child? This is the million dollar question and I spent countless hours wondering what kind of a monster gave birth to me? I remember thinking, "What happened to her", "who hurt her" and "what happened to the woman who cared enough to give birth to me"? How do I live a productive life coming from such torture? How do I treat other people decently?

Chapter IV - Food or Alcohol?

Mom had gotten to the place in her addiction where her options were Food or Alcohol? Poverty was a symptom, not the problem or the reason we did not have food. We did not have food because mom preferred to feed her addiction, rather than feed her kids. Addiction, isolation and darkness consumed her and the only thing she desired to do was live in the fog of intoxication. School provided safety and relief; I could get away from mom and her abuse. Going to school provided me a good hot meal; allowed me a break from abuse and from cooking and cleaning for the family. In Greenville, Mississippi when I was a child, they served full hot and fresh lunch's every day. I can still remember the smell and taste of those fresh homemade rolls. Before I started elementary school, during the regular school year she worked long hours as a housekeeper for a white family. During the summer she left early and returned late working in the cotton field. By the time I was in the first grade she was home every day and her alcoholism was in full-bloom. Her working had little impact on the amount of food in our house. Most days we were very hungry and never had much food in the house. We hustled for food by fishing and catching wild game, but it still was not enough food in the house for all of us to eat.

In the early 1970's before we received food stamps, the government passed out commodity food. Mom would send us to stand in long lines for hours to get commodity foods to eat. It consisted of a 5lb box of cheese, pork and beef in cans and some other processed food. It was not healthy, but it was filling. Later in the 1970's we got approved for food stamps. My neighbors were all very poor people, but most behaved and said they were ashamed of receiving

85

food stamps. They made fun of us for receiving food stamps, but I used to see them at the Department of Human Services office picking up their food stamps. When they saw me they would speed up and walk faster, in an attempt to hide from me. But I never said anything to them, because it did not matter to me, who was and was not getting food stamps. What really mattered to me was that we were not hungry and we could get fed. We always lived in "hunger crisis" it was always a crisis because we were always hungry. Before her addictions took control of her she and my brother JD were both very ashamed of us getting food stamps. But as hungry as we were, I was thankful for food stamps. Poverty made life very difficult, but after food stamps things did initially get a little better. In the beginning she picked up her food stamps, went to the grocery store and purchased food for the family.

Supervision Required

Mom required supervision, because she had gotten to the point where every decision she mad was made around her addictions. Her addictions completely controlled our lives. In the 1970's the Department of Human Services had a standard that they used to provide what they considered a monthly supply for welfare and food stamps for each family and household. We were a family of ten and we received one hundred twenty dollars in cash assistance and about four hundred fifty dollars in food stamps once a month. So if we mismanaged that amount or our food ran out before month's end, we had to wait until the following month to get food stamps again. She was always ashamed of receiving food stamps. But before her addiction took over, she would push through her shame and pride to get up early and go to the Department of Social Services to pick up "her food stamps". She told us they were her food stamps, not ours. In the beginning after receiving her food stamps she went directly to the grocery store and spent most of the food stamps on groceries. However, as her addictions consumed her that soon changed. She asked, "Faye, should I buy food or alcohol"? In that moment I knew for mom, supervision was required, in order for her to do the right thing. This is when I made the decision that I needed to miss school on food stamp day in order to stay home and supervise mom. As her drinking increased, the amount of food in the house decreased.

She kept her addictions feed; she had three a corner store accounts and a corn liquor account, with very little money to pay them off. In order to maintain these addiction accounts she used "her food stamps" to cover her monthly corner store bills. Her need to manage her addiction accounts resulted in less food stamp to buy food, which left less food in the house to eat. Less food in the house brought us back to "hungry crisis" and "hustling for food".

School offered hope and a full meal; I was very happy to go to school every day. I was a very bright and exceptional student in school and I loved going to school, but my survival needs took precedence over my educational needs. Mom had a second grade education, so she never cared for school or valued the importance of getting educated. She would say, "Faye you are dumb and stupid, you might as well not go to school." The only day I wanted to stay home from school was food stamp day that was because she needed to be supervised. Her decision making was very diseased and impaired. She reasoned should I buy "food or alcohol"? She was so wasteful and careless with her food stamps and any form of money she received. If I did not stay home and go with her to the grocery store, we would not have gotten any food to eat. As young as I was, I was now parenting mom, so I was okay with staying home on food stamp day. Food or alcohol was the financial struggle we were having every day of the month, especially on food stamp and check day. Each month I stayed home and went to the Department of Human Services with her or for her. The other reason I wanted to stay at home on food stamp day was because that was the only day of the month that I would get to choose my own meal and be able to prepare it before she got intoxicated. Food stamp day was the only day of the month she woke up and deliberately would not take a drink of alcohol. She knew in order to get her food stamps she had to talk to a Department of Human Services worker, so she would do whatever she needed to do to so that this transaction would occur without a glitch. She was an expert "welfare gamer", who knew the "welfare game" very well and she played it live a fined toned instrument. The "welfare game" was her putting on the appearance of being sober, well groomed and a dedicated parent. She worked really hard at keeping up appearances; because she never wanted anyone to start asking questions that she knew she did not want to or could not answer. She did not want them to know she was an explosive, abusive alcoholic who tortured her kids. She did not want that worker to smell alcohol on her breath, so she did not drink and put gum in her mouth to mask any leftover smells. She was an addict who depended on her food stamps to feed her addiction, so she was not going to do anything to stop her food stamps or welfare check. Therefore she did everything she could to appear to have it together; which included not taking a drink of alcohol before she went to the food stamp office. It was very hard for her not to take a drink of alcohol, because she had the "alcohol shakes". If she did not drink alcohol, her hands shook so bad that she could not hold anything. She would say, "I need a drink of alcohol to steady my nerves. I can't function without an alcohol." In spite of her nerves and hands on food stamp day, she was anxious, but she rose early and went to the food stamp office in order to beat the large crowds. Keeping up appearances to the Department of Human Services was important to her, but getting sober and treating her children right was not important to her.

I realized that my life and circumstances were very different from my classmates. While my classmates were playing jump rope, patty cake, swinging and having great fun. I had so many concerns a young child should have never had to be concerned about. I was at home protecting my siblings; as we struggled to survive. We dodged knives; avoided hot boiled water being thrown at us; spent the night running from fire on paper in her hands, so I would not get burned; and trying to determine if we would live or die. I was also concerned that if my siblings and I did live, we would have to have food to eat, even if we had to sneak and eat that food. Every month on food stamp day, I knew I needed to supervise mom and make sure we had food to eat. Because of mom's addiction and isolation, we had to sneak in the kitchen, prepare the food and hide so we could eat. But if I did not supervise her there would not be any food in the kitchen for us to sneak and eat. I am not saying I was the only kid in the world going through such devastating circumstances, but I knew among my classmates, my situation was rare and unique. Therefore, I stayed home, supervised mom and did exactly what I had to do. I knew I could go to school either later that day or the next day. In spite of my pushy and forceful presence, she got four hundred and fifty dollars in food stamps; she would only spend two hundred dollars at the grocery store for the entire month. I was the one who took the brunt of her torture and abuse, but I was also the one who had the greatest influence over her. She was the most stubborn and strong will person I have ever met, yet she asked me questions to let me know that she was very ignorant and vulnerable at the same time. Twenty hundred dollars out of four hundred fifty was less than half, but two hundred dollars was much more than zero dollars. She feed her addictions with food stamps, but the corner store owners are partially at fault.

It was illegal to buy and sell alcohol to minors and to pay for alcohol and cigarettes with food stamps. The corner store owners in my neighborhoods allowed me a minor to purchase alcohol and cigarettes and they allowed me to pay for them with food stamps. Not only did they do these illegal activities but they would overcharge the poor people in our community each month. These poor customers are the reason these corner store businesses remained open. Mom did not appear to care that she was being overcharged. Her focus was on feeding her addiction and nothing else really mattered. I remember telling her that she was being cheated, but she just told me, "Shut your big mouth, Faye you talk too much," I felt bad for her and our neighbors, but she clearly did not care. Mom would say, "That is the price of doing business on credit."

Chapter V - Hungry, Does Neighbors Know?

Poverty led her to shame, shame led her to addiction and addiction led her to abuse. She didn't care that we were hungry, she said, "Faye, you are hungry, but does the neighbors know that we are poor? Mom received a small welfare check and food stamps to feed us, but she refused to allow us to eat. She would not feed us, but due to her shame she did not want the neighbors to feed us. We were hungry, but she had too much pride to ask the neighbors for assistants. The neighbors knew and talked about it a lot. We were so poor, but in the early days, she was too ashamed to go to the department of social services to pick up her monthly food stamps. It was very confusing to me; sometimes she wanted to go, because she wanted to get drunk early, other times she was too ashamed to go. If she had to go, she went, but if she did not have to go, she would send me. On her shame months she kept me out of school to send me to pick up the food stamps. I was totally okay with this, because she was getting to the point that she preferred to buy alcohol over food. Eventually, the only option was for me to go with her or to go for her. I also knew this was the only day of the month that she would allow me to eat hassle free, as long as I ate before she became intoxicated. The problem was 98% of the time she was intoxicated. If she started drinking before she went to the grocery store, she would never make it to the store. If she did not get to the grocery store on food stamp day, we would not have food for the rest of the month. When she was intoxicated she hated to see us. She would say, "Yack I hate to you coming into the kitchen to bother me." Intoxication meant isolation to the kitchen which meant no food for the children. Once she was intoxicated it was over, she sat in the kitchen, refused to cook for us, let us enter or allow us to eat. Only thing that mattered was her drinking alcohol and smoking cigarettes in the kitchen for days at a time. As each day went on I would ask if I could cook some food for the family, she would just stare at me, with her hand over her mouth, sitting in front of the refrigerator and say "Hell nall you black bitch you can't eat or cook".

Poverty was not the reason we were hungry; her presence meant hunger in my home. At home I was always hungry; never able to satisfy my appetite, because she never allowed us to eat. I tried to avoid the kitchen and her during the day by playing basketball at the park or across the street from our house. I played basketball, but I did not go too far. In spite of her abusiveness I was very protective of her.

I needed to hear her when she called. My childhood daily diet consisted of cheap sweet candy and high carbs; because sweets curved my appetite and carbs made me fill full. I developed a very unhealthy relationship with food.

Even though mom refused to feed us; she did not want the neighbors to know. She was ashamed, but she was prideful. She also did not want any food from the neighbors, because this would have made our poverty real to her. She said, "I hate all those neighbors who get in my business. They are looking at me, talking about me, laughing at me and they are ashamed of me." I was sooooo hungry, I felt like I would faint every day. So when the neighbors offered me food, I was terrified to go to their house to eat. All I could hear was mom threatening me by saying, "You better not let the neighbors know that we are poor and hungry. Faye, I don't care if you starve to death, you better not let anyone know it." This fear was brought on by many incidents that occurred when I was a young hungry kid. I knew she was ashamed of our poverty and about our living conditions. But I did not believe her shame would actually prevent her from feeding her children. It was absolutely important to her how the neighbors viewed her. She lived in constant fear that the neighbors, who were very poor themselves, would find out we were poor and starving. Her fears were more important than feeding her children.

One day I was outside playing by one of our neighbor's house and smelled some Churches Fried Chicken. I was so hungry, as I was most days. My stomach started growling and my mouth started salivating. I knew I wanted some chicken but I knew I could not just go ask them for some chicken. God was working for me that day through my neighbor; all of a sudden the neighbor invited me into her home. She offered me some chicken, of course I quickly and gladly accepted. In that moment I was so happy and I forgot about mom and her threatening's and bullying's. I'm good; I was smiling from ear to ear. Churches Chicken was just as I had dreamed it would be and it was delicious. I ate about three pieces, some mash potatoes and a biscuit. I thought I had died and gone to Churches Chicken Heaven. I was so grateful and thankful to eat it because I had never eaten any Churches Chicken before, but I had smelled it in the neighborhood and saw the commercials on television, so I wanted some so bad. I felt like for the first time I was satisfied, full and well feed. At my house we ate pinto beans in the morning, beans in the afternoon and beans in the evening. My stomach was happy, plus for once, I did not to compete with my six older brothers. I was the first girl born to a family of seven brothers, but they never treated me special. I thought that my brothers should have provided for me first, but that never happened. Growing up in my house I was treated like one of the boys which I hated. There was something really amazing and special about eating Churches Chicken for me. So when the neighbors offered to treat me like a human and to allow me to eat without competing with my animal acting older brothers, in that moment, I felt spectacular. I was glad to accept her invitation. After I was full and satisfied, I remembered mom. I became afraid because she was so unstable. I was not sure if she would understand about me eating at the neighbor's home. So I decided I was not going to tell her that I ate. I was happy, so after I ate, I went straight home. As I approached my house I saw mom standing outside with a belt in her hand. She called me into the house and said, "Faye I received a phone call from the neighbor." My heart started to beat very fast and my hands began to sweat. Mom said, "Juanita called and said you ate Churches Chicken at her home". She quickly lifted the belt in the air and proceeded to beat me until she was tired of beating me. She kept saying, "Faye, didn't I tell you not to take your black ass to other people's houses and eat their food. I don't care if we do not have any food in our house you do not go to the neighbor's house and eat. I am so ashamed of you for eating over there. Now they are going to tell everyone that you are poor and don't have any food to eat". I remember thinking to myself, "we are poor and we don't have any food in our house", but I did not utter those words. I was so afraid of her, but I knew that I should never allow her to find out that I ate food at any ones house ever again. Because I knew the only way I was going to eat was to eat at other people's houses. I also knew I could never eat at Ms. Juanita's house again. I wondered for a second, why did Ms. Juanita help me by feeding me, and then followed that up by calling mom? After that second, I really didn't care why she called. That was a beating that was well worth it. I was not hungry and for one day in my childhood, I did not eat pinto beans. I was full and satisfied. In spite of mom's abusiveness and bullying, I still would sneak and eat at selective people's houses, like Mother Rose and Son Hall, but they had to promise not to tell mom.

Somebody Loved Me

I felt very unloved and alone in my family, but God blessed somebody to love me. I had a pair of community grandparents who loved and valued me a great deal in the Lick Skillet community. As I write and look back at my life, God always provided people to love me, even though I could not value or appreciate it at the time. Those neighbors were Ms. Rosie "Mother Rose" Smith and Mr. Willie "Son" Hall. I met them when I was four years old. Mother Rose was in my life when between four and ten years old. She was my godmother, mentor, guide, counselor and friend. She taught me so much about love, generosity, cooking, cleaning, proper social skills, wise living and life in general. I realize now, that they laid a great foundation for me. I spent countless hours at both places, but the bulk of my time was spent with Mother Rose, because I loved her so dearly. I adored both of them, they were my community grandparents and I was fortunate to know and spend time with them. Mother Rose and Son Hall are two of the greatest influences of my life. Mother Rose was about eighty five years old when I met her and Son Hall was about eighty seven years old. They were clear minded and ready to leave their wealth of knowledge behind for anyone who would listen to them. God knew I would need all the knowledge for the journey ahead, so he blessed me with Mother Rose and Son Hall.

Mother Rose was a very patient woman who first claimed my brother JD, Jr. as her god-son. But later she took me under her wings and shared much of her insightful counsel with me. I feel so grateful to have known both Mother Rose and Son Hall. They provided me with the stability that I clearly lacked at home. I believe part of my childhood safety came because I spent quality time around these two elderly people. As lonely, unloved and hungry as I was, I thank God for mother Rose, because she provided me with friendship, love and food. Mother Rose treated me very special; she allowed me to eat at her house, and when I was late she would wait for me to come and cook for me when I got there. As she cooked, she patiently took time to teach me how to cook. Spending time at Mother Rose's house became the highlight of my days. At home I was one of nine, but at Mother Rose, I was the center of her attention and I still love her for that. Her love and attention made me a very willing subject for her to impart her wisdom. A large part of her generosity was demonstrated when she shared her time and love of knowledge with me. Every day, especially during the summer, I got up early and went to Mother Rose house.

Mother Rose taught me so many things; how to love others; how to be generous; how to forgive; how to be a lady; how to pay close attention to people; how cook; how to clean; and not to let people take advantage of me. She was everything that mom was not. She was very nurturing and lovingly she called me, "Baby". Food preparation, cooking and eating was a great part of our daily fellowship. As I look back I realize that she needed me as much as I needed her. She really loved me and looked forward to me coming over. She was lonely and enjoyed my company as much as I enjoyed her company. I was so fortunate to have shared time and space with her. I felt very blessed and I knew it was rare to sit around for hours and listen to her talk to me. She shared with me story after story from her life experiences. She was a mid-wife in our community and she delivered many of the children from our neighborhood; she also delivered one or two of my brothers. She has had a life-long and very calming impact on my life. She showed me what love and patience looked like. I was so young, but I still knew that this was so valuable to me. She taught me these things during a time that I needed them the most. At the time I did not know how important love and patience would be for me on my life's journey.

She taught me how to value mom. She told me, "Baby, your mom, Celeste is a good woman, but she has had it hard. Always remember she is your mother and you obey her know matter what she does". She gave me story after story of mom. She told me of times before I was born when mom worked hard and the sacrifices she made to raise us. God used Mother Rose to help me overlook and forgive mom of her flaws. She helped me to see that mom did things that she did not want to do, in order to feed us. She stressed the importance of me truly valuing, respecting and honoring mom. She respected mom and she appreciated all the hard work mom did in the early years. She told me about mom crying when her second husband walked out on her and how he left her broke and hungry and with nine children. She helped me to see mom through loving eyes, she valued and respected her, and thereby I began to place value, respect and appreciation on mom. Each day Mother Rose spent time teaching me social skills such as learning how to communicate effectively, talking about boys, discussing current events, planting flowers, gardening, entertaining her friends, cooking some splendid meals from scratch, baking cookies and cakes and many other wonderful things. Mother Rose was so willing to give of herself to me and she was wonderful to me. I know my life is richer and so much better because mother Rose and I spent so much quality time together.

Willie "Son" Hall

Son Hall gave of himself just as freely as Mother Rose, but my time with him was shared with my brother Michael, because Son Hall was Michael's paternal grandfather. Mom never told me who my father was, but she loved Michael's father, so she told him who his dad was. Michael's father was a married Baptist preacher name Lynwood. Lynwood was Son Hall's son, but Lynwood never had anything to do with Michael, but I know that bothered Michael a lot. Michael never spoke of his father and his father never came over to our house. The rumor was Lynwood loved mom and wanted to marry her, but the problem was they were both married to other people. The rumor is that Lynwood was married with a family of his own, but he had a host of outside children. Michael is a mirror image of Lynwood. Son Hall acknowledged Michael as his grandson and clearly loved him very much. I cut short my time at Son Hall's because I did not want to intrude on Michael's time with his grandfather. I still appreciated the time at Son Hall house, listening to him and sharing in his knowledge and insight. He had a swing on his porch, which was designed for social encounters. Some days we would visit him, sit with him, and talk with him. We would swing for hours on his porch swing. Son Hall suffered from very poor health as he aged and he was in and out of the hospital. When he was home, he gave us lots of love, snacks to eat and he freely gave us dollars to go to the store and spend.

The Beginning of My Salvation

When I was sixteen years old my brother, Michael took me with him to the Church of Christ. I obeyed the gospel of Jesus Christ, which completely saved and changed my life. God brought a Christian woman into my life that gave me hope and completely changed my view of people and my outlook on life. I was a junior in high school and in need of hope and a positive role model. I had just been placed back into mom's home after she burned me. I had gotten up and went to church as I did every Sunday morning. However, on this particular Sunday, Carolyn Lee was there visiting Greenville, Mississippi from San Antonio, Texas. She was a young, beautiful, knowledgeable, wise, well-spoken and eloquent sister who I listened to in bible class with great interest and fascination. During the closing discussion Carolyn spoke about God and how He could make the impossible possible in my life. I had never met another person who was so young who possessed the kind of faith in God that Carolyn spoke of. Although I did not know her, I instantly knew God brought her to me to bring me a message of hope. I was suicidal when I met Carolyn and I was contemplating taking my life. But God used Carolyn to change my thinking and provide me with a hope in God that I had never had before.

Carolyn left that Sunday and returned to San Antonio, but I possessed a new hope in God and my life was completely changed forever. My outlook was different, but my mother was more abusive and volatile toward me. One year later in my senior year of high school, I moved to San Antonio, Texas to live with my brother Michael and his wife Reecee. It was too much of a strain for my brother and his young wife, who had one child and another on the way. God blessed me when He allowed Carolyn and her husband Seaburgh to take me into their home. He would allow me to finish my senior year of high school. This was a perfect situation for me. I loved living with Carolyn and her family.

My Break Through

I was seventeen and more suicidal. I spent ninety five percent of my time consumed with self-hatred, worthlessness and death. I wrote death poems and sang the saddest song about dying. One day Carolyn came to me crying. I asked her what was wrong and she said, "I just finished reading your poems and you are thinking about killing yourself aren't you?" I wondered why she was crying, but I said, "Yes I am." She said, "I love you and I don't want you to kill yourself." Her concern, emotion and love for me absolutely shocked me. I had been told by mom all my life, "Faye I hate you." Faye you ain't worth loving." Faye, if your mammie don't love or want you, ain't anybody going to ever love you." Now Carolyn was showing me and telling me something completely different than what mom had conditioned me to believe. Carolyn was crying and felt sadness because of how she felt about me. She hugged me and told me that she loved me. She convinced me that I was special and worth a great deal. Carolyn was the first person that helped me to see that mom was wrong; I was special and worth loving. Carolyn was my break through and she helped me to see life from a totally different perspective. This was the second time that God used Carolyn to save me and change my life; but it was definitely not the last time.

Carolyn was unlike my mother; she was generous, unselfish, nurturing, mentoring, role model, confidant, cheerleader and my best-friend. She was a lady and everything I always wanted to be. She was more than willing to share her time and life with me. She was so unselfish, generous, kind, sensitive, understanding and patient with me. She allowed me space and time to trust in her and she did not push me to emotionally move forward. She nurtured my growth. She was the first person to spend quality time with me. She was the first person to take me shopping and she allowed me to buy and chose whatever clothing I wanted. She purchased everything I needed my senior year of high school. She provided every financial expense that I needed from my senior portraits, cap and grown, wardrobe, earrings and every accessory I needed.

Carolyn was my cheerleader and coach in the hospital during the birth of my first son, Micah Isaiah. My first birth was so difficult; I strained so hard that I ruptured blood vessels in both my eyes. She was there holding my hands, encouraging me not to give up. I was in a military hospital which did not provide me with pain medicine to reduce the pain I was experiencing when I was in labor. I was in labor so long and my pains were so hard that I told Carolyn, "I am in such pain that I want to die." Carolyn said, "Roslyn you can do this, don't give up and don't quit."

Many hours later Micah Isaiah was born and everything worked out very well. She supported me during the birth of my second son, Daniel Jeremiah. My third child and first daughter, I named Carolyn Joyce in honor of Carolyn.

Before I met her; mom had the greatest negative impact on my life; but Carolyn had the greatest positive impact on my life. She has been such a powerful influence that I can't remember not having her in my life. She is and always has been my family. Carolyn and I are closer today than we ever were. Over the years she has played the same role in the life of my three children that she played in my life. She has been the only real grandma to my kids; even though they call her Aunt Carolyn. Being a single parent, I am thankful for her, because my three children always had the best clothes and shoes, because Aunt Carolyn has always sent large gift boxes to us no matter where we lived.

Chapter VI - The Seizures

The seizures were my first indication of mom's mortality. Until she started having seizures I thought she could drink as much as she wanted to and it would have no effect on her. Now I was witnessing all that change. I was seeing how much her addiction was destroying and taking control of her body. For years she made it clear that her goal was death, so she did not seem to care. It was 1979 and she was having seizures every other day, so she was in and out of the hospital. Her doctors kept pumping her with medication and telling her to stop drinking. She simply refused to listen to them. I told her that she was killing herself, but she told me, "I am the mother and you are the child, you can't tell me anything".

Her first few seizures terrified me; because I had never witnessed anyone have a seizure. Although I had seen people on television experience seizures, it was very hard watching mom have seizures. I had spent years watching her demeanor and personality change drastically, but I had not seen her experience any physical health problems. She had always consumed various types of alcohol and in large amounts, but now she was also taking many different prescription medications with the same amount of alcohol consumption. On the label of each medication bottle there was a warning stating, do not use this medication with alcohol. I noticed that she was mixing alcohol and prescription medications without any side effects or problems. I often told her, "You are not supposed to take these medications and consume alcohol". She would say, "Those doctors don't know what they are talking about, it ain't gonna hurt me". I guess she felt the medical restrictions did not apply to her since she had not had any negative side effects from mixing alcohol and prescription medication for years. I was convinced that when it came to drinking alcohol and prescription medications, she was invincible and could do as she pleased. Mom was only in her early 40's, but due to her addictions she was aging rapidly. Each day I watched my young, beautiful, and vibrant mother, who was once 5'6, 160lbs dwindle down to a 95lb little old lady. I saw her drink until she threw up, urinated and defecated in her clothes. She kept those soiled clothes on for days at a time. I spent my childhood picking and cleaning up behind her. She had become more like a wild animal that could no longer care for itself. She stayed so intoxicated that she did not know whether she was dead or alive. Yet each day she repeated this destructive behavior. Mom never appeared to care about the damage she was doing to herself or to those around her. Her focus was getting high or becoming intoxicated.

On the day mom had her first seizure, we had just moved to the north end of Greenville, Mississippi to a new neighborhood. Prior to this move, I had become accustomed to her drinking alone and isolating herself from the family and the outside world that seemed to trouble her so much. I was thirteen years old and we had always lived from one shot-gun house after another, but now we were moving into a three bedroom house. The address was 238 Witts Lane. This was the largest and best house we ever lived in during my childhood. Mom always complained that all our previous houses were too small, too crowded or how ashamed she was of the house. She was never satisfied and she was the most miserable person I have ever met. She never appeared to be happy, or at peace; she lived in a constant state of agony. 238 Witts Lane was a three bedroom house that she handpicked. Experience had taught us that we should allow her to pick the house, because she was going to complain no matter what happen, so it was best to let her choose. If she chose she could only blame herself. For years we had lived with her constant nagging and blame shifting. With a new house, I hoped she would stop drinking, join Alcoholics Anonymous, strive to be happier, and mostly I hoped she would stop abusing us. This house supposedly represented the kind of house that mom talked about living in for years. In 1975, my brother JD joined the United States Army. He made a promise to mom to buy her a nice home. This was the promise made by an unstable and lying kid. JD never intended to keep the promise he made to mom. Mom was devastated that JD did not keep his promise. This was another reason for her to drink more. Now 1979, four years after the promise, JD was no longer in the Army and he had not purchased her a house. Mom said, "Other people's children love them, buy them houses and takes care of them, but not my children". She had forgotten for the last four years he sent her an allotment check each month, but she did not save any part of that money. She drank it up. She was so filled with self-pity she could not see that he kept his promise to her the best way he knew how. He sent her two hundred dollars per month for four years, but she was so irresponsible that she did not save any of that money. She was so selfish, ungrateful and so far gone in her addiction, that no one could reason with her. In her intoxication, she feed on bitterness and misery. JD, Larry, Carl, Danny and Michael had all joined the United States Military and she was receiving five allotment checks every month. She wasted all that money as well. I reminded her that she should be more grateful, because ten of us lived in a one bedroom shot-gun house. Now it was only four of us living in a three bedroom house. But alcoholism had destroyed any hope of good within her. She was receiving more money than ever and we lived in a beautiful new home, but she was more miserable than ever before. I soon learned it was never about the houses we lived in but about her misery that she could never shake.

As we tried to settle into our new neighborhood mom initially isolated herself as she had always done, but eventually met Ms. Glendora Miller, who befriended mom. Ms. Miller and her husband Gene were both alcoholics. They were very social and good people. Mom was doing what active social alcoholics do which was to seek out other alcoholics to drink with and to get intoxicated with. I was so grateful that she was getting out of the kitchen. She started visiting the Miller's home on a regular basis. At first the Millers lived around the corner from us but after a few months they moved next door to us. Ms. Miller was a wonderful person; what I appreciated most was her personality was mild, calm and consistent. Her personality did not change no matter how much alcohol she consumed. I really loved and appreciated the Miller family for many reasons. They were very generous and kind hearted folks. Ms. Miller never appeared to get tired of kids in and out of her house. She kept her refrigerator stocked with plenty of food and did not mind me eating as much as I liked. This was quite different from my home, where mom guarded the food and did not allow us to eat it. They thought I was very bashful and quiet. I had been conditioned through beatings not to eat at other people's homes. They used to tease me about not eating at their home, but eventually I began to feel more comfortable, so I ate. I was more afraid that mom was going to find out and beat me for eating. As I now look back, I see God using the Miller family to feed me. I spent countless hours in their home and they did not mind me visiting, eating and hanging out at their home. The Millers had five children, four daughters and one son. One of their older daughters, Brenda and I became the best of friends. Brenda was ten years older than I, but we connected like we were sisters, but born to different mothers. As a matter of fact, I was the maid of honor in Brenda's wedding. Despite Ms. Miller's struggle with alcohol she was in every other way the complete opposite of mom. She was very affectionate, warm, open, loving, and very generous. She was the perfect hostess; she enjoyed buying alcohol and inviting others over to drink with her. Mom the recluse had a new friend and I was happy. Ms. Miller opened her home and invited mom over to hang out with her on a daily basis. Mom always messed up any friendships she had ever been involved in. I was hoping and praying that Ms. Miller's friendship and influence would help mom to treat us much better. Ms. Miller's personality was amazing to me. She seemed to love and adore her family no matter what they did.

One afternoon while mom was visiting and drinking alcohol with Ms. Miller, they were talking and having a good time for hours. All of a sudden mom's eyes rolled back in her head, her head went back, she fell to the floor, her body stiffened up, she began to shake and twitch. She bit her tongue repeatedly, her body took on a straight board like position and she convulsed repeatedly. I was thirteen years old, terrified and begin to think, "Mom is dying and I cannot help her" I began to cry and call out to her as she lay there. I screamed, "Mom come back, please come back". I remember feeling so helpless and scared that she would not make it through that seizure. I did not know what was happening to her, because at the time I did not know exactly what a seizure was or what caused it. They called 911, the ambulance was dispatched to the Miller's home and mom was taken to the hospital. She was admitted into Delta Regional Hospital, treated, given more medication and after a few days released with the instructions, "Ms. Rogers, stop drinking, you are destroying your liver. Please do not mix alcohol, prescription medications and seizure medication". Mom said to the doctor, "I only drink a beer every now and then". The doctors had done her blood work, so they knew her alcohol blood levels. She came home, but she never discussed the seizure, the alcohol or the damage that she was doing to her body or to her children. From this day forward she continued to mix alcohol and prescription medications, so her seizures increased. She frequented the hospital so much that the doctors knew her by name. I was completely honest with her doctors about her drinking, but they did not really care about her or her family. I believed with medical and social service interventions, many problems we later faced would have never happened. After the first couple of seizures she said she was ashamed, so she retreated back into the kitchen and became reclusive just as before. Now she became more of a high risk to harm self and others. Due to the uncertainty of the seizures I was more afraid to leave her unattended. I knew I would be tortured by her but her safety was more important than my own. I never wanted to come home and discover that she had a seizure or had fallen and really hurt herself. She constantly had new bumps, bruises, cuts, scratches, and pin holes all over her body. I had become accustomed to seeing her battered and bruised up. These bruises never deterred or altered her drinking habits; she made excuses why her skin looked the way that it did. She told me "I stopped looking at myself in the mirror many years ago because I no longer liked what I see looking back at me".

Chapter VII - The Burn!!!!

Due to her shame around the seizures mom pulled back from Ms. Miller and retreated back to the reclusive drinking in the kitchen. This made me sad, because most days of my childhood were spent in protective and survival mode, trying to protect my siblings and me from mom. Her sole mission appeared to be to hurt and destroy her children physically, verbally, mentally, emotionally and psychologically. She was an alcoholic who was explosive and volatile. My childhood was marked by her torture, abuse and horror on a daily basis. Every day of my childhood was very memorable, but one day and one event changed the entire course of my life. This particular early morning, I had spent the previous night running from her, because she had been chasing me with a knife, as she had so many nights before. The next morning I was totally exhausted. As I had been so many times before, I was praying, hoping and thinking that if I sneak in, maybe she won't be able to hear me and I could get a few hours of sleep, before the war started again. I opened the front door as quietly as I could; tip-toed inside and tried to ease onto the living room sofa. I said to myself, "ok she did not hear me come inside of the house." I was so exhausted, yet I was feeling such great relief that I actually got into the house without any incident from her and without hearing her yell at me as I entered the door. I listened to hear for her to either yell or walk toward me, but I only heard silence. After only a few minutes I drifted off to sleep on the living room sofa. For a split second, I heard her moving around in the kitchen. She was so intoxicated that she was sitting in the kitchen talking out of her head, yet cursing me out. She was in and out of consciousness. Somewhere between me drifting off to sleep and waking up in terrible pain; she boiled a pot of hot water and poured it over my body. It was about 2am; I felt my body on fire and realized very hot water falling all over my body. I woke up screaming and yelling in agony and anguish, crying out to my mom asking her "what have you done to me and why did you burn me"? Mom looked at me, with rage in her eyes, then turned her face away from me and said, "If you were not such a fast, black whore I would not have burned you. Now who is going to help you now"? She staggered back into the kitchen, where she spent the rest of the night and resumed her drinking.

This was the longest night of my life; I thought morning would never come. I spent the next couple of hours waiting for daylight to appear. While I laid there in agony I had what felt like a lifetime to think and pray about my life. I prayed to God for direction as to what to do next? It was not just about me, even though I was the one burned; but what was going to happen to my two younger siblings? I looked at my burned left arm – as it throbbed, blistered, and boiled. I was in absolute agony. My emotions ranged from angry, disappointed, scared, self-pity, sadness, uncertainty and revenge. I honestly did not know what to do. Mom had systematically isolated us from all our friends and family; so I was not sure who to turn to, what to do or where to go? The police had been to our home countless times and all our neighbors knew we were being abused, but absolutely no one offered to help us. I had no hope that any of them would even care, needless to say, try to help us. I felt so unloved, unwanted and alone. I spent the rest of the night praying about what my next move should be? I was only fifteen years old; the only family I knew was my cousin Correen, and my Aunt Lillie; and the only friends were moms drinking buddies from the neighborhood. Mom and cousin Correen got along like vinegar and oil. They absolutely hated one another. I did not feel very confident or comfortable that I could turn to or depend on her. Mom took great confidence and pride in saying, "Faye I hate you and no one will ever love you". Now I was burning and in pain, so I thought to myself, "If mom does not care than no one really cares about me." I thought about calling my brothers, but I did not know how to get in contact with them. I had nine siblings, seven older brothers and two younger siblings. My seven older brothers were all away in the military or in the streets doing their own thing. They had demonstrated that they were not concerned about what mom was doing to us or how she was mistreating us. They had witnessed her abuse of me, but often minimized it and never intervened to prevent or stop her. I watched my brothers leave home, one after the other, but they never looked or reached back to help us. Therefore my younger siblings and I were left at the mercy of God and in the dangerous care of our mother. As the years went by mom's drinking increased and her abuse against us got progressively worse. In spite of this my older brothers never came back to help my younger siblings or me. I was convinced that my brothers did not care about us, so I did not call them. Yes, my two younger siblings and I felt totally alone and helpless. Finally after what seemed like a lifetime passed, now it was 6am. I gathered my younger brother, Kenny and younger sister, Sandra and we left mom's house. After much agony I felt the only place I could go was to my cousin Coreen's house.

Only One Who Helped!!

As I laid there waiting for morning to come I thought about Cousin Correen who was she really? Cousin Correen was a collection of all the negative personalities I had witnessed between mom, Aunt Darling and Aunt Lillie. Correen was at least seven times worse than all my relatives combined. She was a religious drug and alcohol addict, who was mentally unstable. She used pcp, cocaine, marijuana, alcohol and everything she could get her hands on. She grew

137

up in Greenville, but she had moved to Michigan.
Now she, her third husband Leroy and her two
children (Carl and Angela aka Cookie) from a
previous marriage, had moved back to Greenville
from Michigan. Since arriving back to Greenville, she
had assaulted her grandma Lillie and physically
destroyed her house. She assaulted and threw a
bucket of urine in the face of Aunt Darling. She
stabbed herself in front of me and blamed it on her
husband Leroy. She eventually murdered Leroy and
she went to prison, but was released. She hated her
own kids and cared less about them than mom or her
sisters. She beat her son, Carl, made him take a bath
and soap himself down, then get out the bath tub and
she would meet him at the bathroom door with an
extension cord in her hand and beat him again while
he was naked.

Mom was one extreme of psychotic and cousin Correen was the other extreme. I am not sure if my family's addictions led to their psychosis or if their psychosis led them to become addicts. Correen lived her life in strange unstable emotional and psychotic cycles. She rotated from religious fanatic, to alcohol and drug addiction to sobriety and back to addiction within a few months. One day she would be playing "Oh how I love Jesus" very loud on her stereo, but the next day she was high and would be playing the blues song "It is Cheaper to Keep Her". She was very unstable. One moment she was an adult, the next moment she was a three year old child crying, the next moment she was very combative and ready to fight. She repeated my family's dysfunctional pattern of alcohol and drug addiction, physical abuse and mental cruelty. She married her first husband in Mississippi, when she was very young. Her husband was physically abusive to her, similar to the way her grandfather was to her grandmother Lillie. Grandma Lillie had shot and murdered her abusive husband many years earlier. But the difference was Correen provoked her abuser to fight her. She appeared to take great delight and joy in administering pain on her abuser and making him or her suffer great agony and anguish. For example, her first husband beat her, so she poured acid all over his body, forced him to lay there being tortured by her and later she killed him. She was incarcerated, but she pleaded insanity and because they had a documented history of domestic assault, she went to prison for a few years and was soon released. After her release from prison, her Grandma Lillie contacted our family in Michigan, told them her situation and they agreed that Correen could come to Michigan. She purchased her a Grey Hound bus ticket and shipped her to Battle Creek, Michigan to live with other relatives. After she arrived in Michigan she quickly discovered the same family patterns of alcohol and drug addiction existed there. She was already mentally unstable and an alcoholic, now in Michigan she was introduced to and started using pcp, cocaine and many other drugs. While in Michigan Correen met her second husband, James and they married in Battle Creek, Michigan. James was also abusive. Correen and James had two children, Carl and Angela aka Cookie. James and Correen spent most of their time fighting, until she saved enough money to leave him and she returned to Greenville, Mississippi.

She returned to Greenville, Mississippi with her two children and her third husband name Leroy. My family was devastated that Correen was returning to Greenville. My family hoped that while she was in Michigan she had changed and become more mentally stable, gotten sober, and matured. Unfortunately, time did not heal Correen or the open wounds that existed between our families. As wishful as this thinking may have been, it was not realistic or true. The sad reality was so much worse than my family could have ever imagined.

Knowledge is power and I had lots of knowledge in my mind about cousin Correen, I was only a fifteen year old kid who was in a desperate situation and in need of help. I was burned and I was still dealing with a situation that I needed adult guidance to maneuver through. I had no clue about going to the hospital or that I needed to go to the hospital. Mom burned me, made fun of my injury, blamed me for that burn and dared me to find someone to help me. Unstable or not Correen had always treated me nice and always seemed to genuinely love me. In spite of all the harm she did to everyone else, she treated me a little better than she treated others. Maybe God allowed me to have someone that I could turn to when mom completely betrayed me. Correen always welcomed me and opened her home to me. She washed, pressed and combed my hair ever since she returned from Michigan. She gave me money from time to time. Truth was, in spite of all she had done and all the negatives I heard about her, I really liked Correen. I always thought my family never really gave her a chance. I felt she was a sad, misunderstood and broken person. As far as I was concerned, Correen was my only option. As I said before she and mom hated each other. Correen always had her own agenda, which most of the time was motivated by money. I am not sure why she was motivated by money, but she was no different than the rest of my family. As a matter of fact, maybe she was better than the rest, because she was open and honest about the way she was. They did the same things as cousin Correen, but they were more discrete about what they did or who they told about what they did. Mom burning me provided opportunity for Correen's financial (welfare check and food stamps) agenda that had not presented itself before. Mom's burning me seemed to motivate Correen to be extra nice, if for no other reason than to get back at mom. She was the only family who seem willing to help my siblings and me. Correen always seemed to be in competition with mom, but I did not realize how much she hated mom, until mom burned me. Again, despite their differences, unlike mom, Correen responded to my injuries in a genuine, loving and caring way or so I thought.

As we (Kenny, Sandra and I) arrived at her house I was still crying, showed her my burned arm which was still aching, swelling and blistering. She said,

"Faye what happen to you?" I said, "Mom burned me." Correen did not hesitate to help me. She jumped into action. I had gone in mom's purse and took our medical cards so we could go straight to the hospital. After I told Correen how much pain I was in she still waited and made me suffer all that pain, until the Department of Human Services opened. She took me to the Department of Human Services before she took me to the hospital. This was the first time I noticed that she had her own financial (welfare and food stamps) agenda. It was clearly more important for her to get some kind of financial compensation for whatever trouble I had brought to her life. She had an opportunity to do a great service for my family, but she was driven by revenge, greed and was more interested in sticking it to mom, than assisting me through my horrendous process. I was very tired of being abused and living in the home of my torturous mom. Now I was caught in a trap between two insane women that hated one another. I took a chance with Correen to allow my adult cousin to step up and do great good and help me. But she was more interested in paying mom back for some sick problems they had since childhood. Little did I know cousin Correen was about to make my life much, much worse. I found myself in the middle of a tug-a-war between two women who hated each other so much that my pain and well-being was lost in the mist of their hatred. The real fight was not over me, but over the little welfare money and the food stamps that the state paid them to provide care for children. How could two women love money so much and love children so little?

The System

Correen was surprised when the Department of Human Services took immediate, but very poor action. They immediately removed my two younger siblings and me from mom's home and placed us in emergency state custody. We were placed in the Salvation Army shelter in Greenville, Mississippi. The Salvation Army shelter exposed us to a couple of decent people, but also exposed us to so many wild things and wild people. Prior to going to the shelter I was taken to the hospital where I was diagnosed with third degree burns. I spent the next year in and out of rehabilitation and physical therapy to treat my burn. I was not referred to a psychologist or psychiatrist. One of the best things that happened was they placed mom in the Mississippi State Mental Institution in Jackson, Mississippi for the clinically insane. She became even more bitter and hateful toward me. She demonstrated to me that she had no real desire to take responsibility for her actions or to change her behavior. For example in front of the hospital staff she pretended that she loved me and was not angry at me. As soon as they walked away she would say, "Faye I hate you, you no good black whore, it is your fault that I am in this place." I was told by my brother Carl that he had the courage to place her in the Mississippi State Mental Institution as a result of what she did to me. Carl said, "I am glad that I put her away, because she was wrong for burning you, Faye, but I am struggling with that decision because the brothers might be mad at me for putting her away." I was not mad, but very relieved. Carl was my new hero who finally had the courage to take action against mom. I was so irritated with my brothers and I thought I hated them. I thought to myself, what difference does it make to them? For years mom had tortured, abused, neglected and emotionally abandoned us and my brothers never uttered a word. All of a sudden my older brothers who left home and never looked back to help my siblings or me had an opinion. They wanted their voice heard regarding whether or not mom should be placed and remain in the Mississippi State Mental Hospital for the insane. Where were they the many days and nights I cried for help and ran from knives, broomsticks and hot water? They either did not care or were too ashamed to come back and help us, but now they had an opinion and a voice about a decision that was going to change the entire course of my life. They had been driven by shame and fear for years and too embarrassed to tell other people that their mother was insane. My siblings and I were the ones directly impacted by whether she stayed or was released from the mental hospital, but no one asked us what we thought was the best thing to do. This was so unfair because they all had their own lives and families.

None of them lived with us therefore they should not

be the one to make the decision. Unfortunately, the

Department of Human Services, cousin Correen, my

older brothers or my mother did not have our best

interest at heart, so they all decided that she should

not have to stay in the mental hospital. She stayed in

the mental hospital only a few days. My brother

Michael was seventeen years old when mom signed

papers so he could leave home to join the United

States Air Force before he turned eighteen years old.

Michael said, "I left home early because mom is

driving me crazy and if I stay here I will kill her."

Michael and I had agreed that we were not going to

do like our older brothers who left home and didn't

look back. We both promised that we would come

back and rescue whoever was left under mom's

destructive care. Unfortunately Michael did not keep

his end of our agreement. He left home, became engaged and got married. Michael and my older brothers collectively lead the charge to have her discharged from the mental hospital. This was the worst move they could have made for my siblings and me. I was so angry at Michael and all my brothers, but I especially felt abandoned by Michael.

Michael drove from Greenville, Mississippi to Jackson, Mississippi to have mom released from the mental hospital. Meanwhile we were still in emergency foster care at the Salvation Army shelter. As I said there was a couple of good employees at the Salvation Army shelter, but for the most part we were poorly supervised by the staff. It was supposed to be a locked and highly supervised facility, however whenever I wanted to I slipped away from the shelter. I only wanted to check on mom. I felt strongly that since all my life I had taken care of her, I needed to go and check on her, because she was so broken and fragile. I knew I could not turn off my love and concern for her even though she burned me and I was placed out of the home. In spite of her torturing me, my love and concern for her overpowered any fear that I may have felt toward her. Part of the state agreement for her release in order for us to be returned home was for her to get sober, work an Alcoholics Anonymous program and to take parenting classes. I wanted to see for myself whether or not she was working her program. I grew up with her, so I knew how beautiful, charming and polished she could come across to the Department of Human Services, if she wanted too. The problem may have been Greenville, Mississippi had a bunch of overworked and underpaid social workers, who did not have the time or energy to make unannounced home visits, so my social worker relied on my abuser to tell her the truth, but mom was not going to tell the truth.

It was convenient that the Salvation Army shelter was only a few blocks from mom's house. The first time I slipped away from the shelter I ran all the way home. As I approached the house, I noticed that the front door was wide open, so I went inside the house. I saw mom sitting on the living room sofa slumped over and I noticed that she was clearly intoxicated out of her mind. I was moved with compassion for her and I started to cry. I said, "Mom are you okay" even though I knew she was far from okay. She pulled her head up appearing to be in a fog of drunkenness said with her muffled sounding voice, "Fayeeeee, is that you"? In that moment I knew The Department of Human Services, cousin Correen, my older brothers and mom had failed our family. Their concern was not lifting mom out of destruction or doing what was in the best interest of my siblings or me, but each one had his own agenda. There were no parenting classes, AA meetings, alcohol and drug counseling, mental health therapy, life coaching or anything else for mom or the family. Why did they remove us? What was the real purpose of taking us from one destructive environment to only place us in even more destructive environment? No one in authority ever showed any real concern for us and they never asked me "What happened in your home?" My life was a complete mess; I spent a great deal of time regretting I went to cousin Correen and to the Department of Human Services. Though I was only fifteen years old, I knew that I needed help; it was unfortunate that all the adults did the wrong thing.

The Salvation Army shelter was filled with many kids, like my siblings and me. Those kids had already been exposed to physical, mental, and sexual abuse, prior to their arrivals at the shelter. Many of them were already child molesters in the making. I remember one young girl who had been sexually abused since she was two years old. Every free moment she had she used the bathroom plunger and the broom or mop handles as sex tools. My siblings and I were initially placed in the shelter together, but that was only for thirty days, we were then separated into different foster homes. Every morning I woke up I experienced guilt, loneliness, Isolation, abandonment, betrayal, and emptiness. Guilt is the emotion I experienced the most. Mom blamed me and because the Department of Human Services, my older brother and cousin Correen had made my life so much worse, I blamed myself. These emotions I felt at home with mom, but I did not experience the torture and abuse in the shelter. I felt like no one really cared about my siblings or the emotions we were feeling. I remembered the words of mom, "If your own mammie hate you, than why would anyone else love your black and ugly ass" This was so traumatic for me; if I really think about it, the pain is just as real today, as it was back then. My experiences in those devastating and unstable environmental circumstances caused me not to trust anyone and not to feel comfortable anywhere. As a result, I have never really felt at home anywhere. As kids we never experienced peace, safety or security, nor did we sleep completely through a full night without some type of abuse from mom. Similar to what mom experienced, loneliness has always been one of my closest companions.

As I said my siblings and I were initially removed and placed together in the Salvation Army shelter. We stayed in the shelter for thirty days, and then we were separated and placed in different foster homes. My two younger siblings were placed with cousin

Correen, but I was placed with my half-sister, Janet. The social worker at the Department of Human Services wanted to know my father's name and if I knew how he could be located? I told her that I did not know my father, but it was a man named JD Rogers whose name on my birth certificate. But rumor had it that he was not my father. I explained to the social worker that mom never told me anything about my father. I did not know JD or the man that the streets told me was my father. I told her that JD did have a daughter name Janet who lived in Metcalf, Mississippi. I shared that Janet had in recent months searched and found us. I did not know Janet very well, because I had only spoken with her a couple of times over the phone. This social worker was either lazy, busy or just didn't care, so without any investigations, she placed me with Janet. We did not know each other; she was very mentally unstable and moody. She was only ten years older, but she had two children of her own. She was struggling with some very difficult personal issues, all of which made it impossible for her to raise a teenager. I was a teenager who needed a stable home environment, which contained patient and loving foster parents. I was with her only about three months and she wanted me out of her house. Janet's moods were so unstable that she clearly needed medication to balance them. Most days I did not know if she was coming or going or if her mood was up or down. My placement with Janet lasted three months and after that I was placed in a girl's group home, like the shelter, only a few blocks from mom's house.

My younger siblings were not doing much better with cousin Correen. One of the many nights when mom was intoxicated, she decided she was ready for Kenny and Sandra to come home without the courts permission of course. Mom arrived at her house and demanded that she give her back Kenny and Sandra. Correen had waited all her life for this opportunity to give mom a taste of her own medicine. She was the foster parent, so she believed that she had the law on her side. If she wanted this to end peaceably, all she had to do was call the police and have mom removed. That is not the way she handled this situation. While Kenny and Sandra watched helplessly as Correen and her son, Carl attacked, stumped and beat mom so bad that when she came to court, we could barely recognize her.

Court Appearance

Shortly after the beating we were scheduled to appear in family court. My social worker picked me up and brought me to court. I was excited to go to court because I got to see mom, Kenny and Sandra. As I approached the court house I saw who I thought was mom, but because she had been beat so badly, I could barely recognize her. She was standing outside, so I ran over to hug her, but she refused to hug me. Because of what happened at Correen's she was more distant and angry at me than ever before. She blamed me for what they did to her. She said, "Faye, I hate your black, ugly ass. You caused all these problems for me. This would have never happened if you had not gotten the welfare involved." I tried again to hug her, but she refused my hug. I was standing close enough to her and I could smell alcohol on her breath. I knew she had been drinking, but the social worker would not hold mom accountable or force mom to get help. It just appeared to me that the social worker did not care about me or my family. The smell of alcohol on mom's breath and the cold rejection of my love, confirmed for me that she was clearly still angry at me and still blamed me for her burning me. I tried again to hug mom, but she stood there looking at me with disgust in her eyes toward me. Noticing my three rejected attempts, the social worker forced mom to hug me. The social worker grabbed my arm, pulled me from her right side toward mom, and then she pulled mom from her left side toward me, now mom and I were face-to-face. I was feeling hopeful and glad that mom would surely want to hug me now, especially in front of the social worker. I smiled, opened and reached my arms out to hug her, but she still refused to hug me and pulled pull away from me. However, the social worker put her hand on moms back and squashed the two of us together to force her to hug me. Even though the social worker pushed us together and tried to force mom to hug me, mom kept her hands straight down by her side and her body remained stiff as a board. In that moment, I felt mom's hatred toward me and I really wish the social worker would have saw that mom hatred me, but the social worker completely missed it. Mom's hatred toward me was obvious, but for whatever reason, the social worker never picked up on it. Mom refused to work her program, because the social worker did not hold her accountable. No matter where I was in foster care, I always made secret trips to mom's house to check on her. On every visit I made to her, she was always intoxicated. She did not get sober, never went to AA meetings, did not attend therapy nor did she go to parenting classes. Nevertheless one year later we were out of foster care and placed back home. Only now things were worse for me.

Convinced that she was right and based on the actions of cousin Correen, the Department of Human Services, my older brothers and her own, mom did absolutely nothing but get one year older and grow bitterer toward me. Since I was wrong and she was right, I was punished by her the rest of the days of her life. Life only got worse for me at my return home. Because she was not held accountable for her actions she not only blamed me for her burning me, but now she felt justified in burning me. After the social worker left mom said, "You black whore, you brought the welfare authorities into my home and I am going to get you for that". She was more self-destructive than prior to burning me and she was more out of control in her explosive and volatile behavior. Her drinking increased and she abused me more than ever before. She would say, "Faye I dare you to go tell anyone, because I will kill you and call you". I was more terrified of her than ever before, but I was not going to go to the authorities. I was now a year older and trying to buy my time until I was old enough to rescue my siblings and myself. I did not trust the authorities, because they had totally let my family down and we completely were swept under the proverbial social services carpet. I was more afraid for my younger siblings than I was for myself. They were four and five years younger than I was, so they were the true victims of mom's madness. It was better that her torture, violence, abuse, rage and bitterness be aimed at me rather than at them. My younger siblings were my two babies and they never stood a chance with the madness of mom. So I knew if I took the brunt of her abuse than they did stand a chance of successfully surviving.

Chapter VIII - Big and Botly (fat)

The names I remember most were **big, botly, black whore and ugly.** I was not sure exactly that botly was a word, but to mom it definitely was a word.

Botly meant big and fat. It was one of the many negative ways mom referred to me. Childhood was a confusing time for me, because I believed I wanted to obey and honor mom, but I also wanted her to honor and respect me. I knew it was wrong to ignore your parent, but I wanted her to call me by the name she gave me at birth, not the many negative names she called me while she was intoxicated. For the first thirty two years of my life I did not feel like I was worth anything. She would say, "Faye you are a big, botly, black and ugly whore. You are coming and I am going. You still have your youth, but I do not and I hate you for that." I knew she was consumed by self-hatred. She was struggling with the reality that her addiction was destroying her beauty, because she often said, "I stopped looking in the mirror years ago, because I don't recognize that woman in the mirror". I was so overwhelmed by the many cruel things she said to me that I did not know what to do.

Food deprivation, a diet filled with high carbs and sweets and playing basketball every day, made my body muscular and very lean. My body appeared to be a lot healthier than it actually was. Whenever I got a lot of compliments of any kind they threatened mom and she became even angrier at me. Since she had to be the center of attention at all cost, she was not okay with anyone giving the attention that once focused on her to me. The more they complimented me, the more she was threatened and saw me as her enemy. I did know that she had become more insecure and doubtful of herself; her addiction and isolation had robbed her of so many things and her self-worth was one of those things. Her diseased mind had caused her to become jealous of me, which made her project her self-hatred onto me. Through the disease of addiction, I became enemy number one and she targeted me through torture and abuse. She had such a distorted body image that my body and weight became an obsession for her.

Addiction and isolation destroyed any true self-image and social skills, she may have once possessed. She had become a social misfit. It was unfortunate that she was so insecure and incapable of seeing her physical beauty and her real beauty. She was and still is one of the most physically beautiful women I have ever known. She had her choice of as many men as she wanted, but she chose men she could control and manipulate very easily. In spite of the fact that she spent most of her time in the kitchen away from us she did come out to entertain the men who came to visit her. She was physically captivating so these men thought they were getting the total package and a real gift. Mom was quite charming;

she was very beautiful, 5'6 and slim; appeared very quiet, well spoken, and was very pleasing to their eyes. Things were great as long as she managed to keep them at a distance. They found her beautiful and very challenging. For a while she controlled the relationship and they only saw her when she wanted to see them. Eventually, she compromised all of her control and allowed a couple of them to spend the night. She could only keep up appearances for a little while, because the beast in her was bound to come out.

As long as she kept them away from the house and controlled the relationship, everything was wonderful. Once she let them spend the night they got to see the real Celeste. Once she intoxicated, her rage could not be controlled, so she attacked them just like she attacked me. They got to see the real Celeste, fangs and all. When they saw her attack me, two of them tried to intervene on my behalf, but to the demise of their relationship with mom. One of these men saw her attack me and he told her, "Celeste, why do you treat Faye so bad, she is a smart and beautiful girl". Mom without any hesitation said, "You must want her for yourself", why are you taking up for that black whore, she ain't worth nothing". On another occasion, she became very angry at me and began to curse, scream and yell at me. Her friend said to her, "Celeste, you should not mistreat Faye, you have a good daughter. She stays home, cleans the house, and does not give you any trouble". Mom said "Do you like her better than you like me, then get the hell out of my house". I was very careful not to hang around the house when she and her men came around, because she disturbingly saw me as some kind of competition. She was quick to tell her men, "You just using me to get to my daughter. Oh you

want to sleep with her and you want her for yourself."
She was so diseased and twisted in her thinking. The
men that were perverts, she did not protect me from,
but the two who genuinely tried to protect me, she ran
away from.

Visitors were extremely rare. Usually the only visitors
were her men. Whenever they did come she insulted
me in front of that visitor. She was attempting to
compete with me and make herself look better in the
eyes of her men. She did not care who was present
when she verbally abused me. Calling me a big,
botly, black and ugly whore was one of her favorite
sports. She did not say anything unless it was
negative and destructive. In her diseased state, she
withheld food from me to prevent my body from
changing and developing. She believed that food was
to be preserved, stored, saved or even rotten, before
it was to be eaten by her children. She said, "I love to

see the refrigerator full, but I hate to see y'all eating any of my food. If I did go in the kitchen she said, "get out of here, Yack, you big and botly whore." She was diseased and never allowed me to eat food, because she thought I was too big and botly.

"Faye, you are big and botly, ugly and no man is going to ever want you". Due to her drinking she was completely wasting away. She had dwindled down to 90lbs. Because she saw her body fading; in her eyes I was young, healthy and beautiful. Since she was looking at me through distortion; watching her beauty and youth fade, she saw me as the biggest threat in her life. It was these constant threats that drove her to torture and abuse me for thirty two years. She was so diseased that when she looked at me, she did not see her daughter, but her enemy. She would say, "Faye, you are coming and I am going and I hate you for that." I tried to make her feel better about herself by telling her how beautiful I thought she was. But it made her angrier for me to be nice to her. She would say, "Faye, you are a liar. How could you possibly love me the way I treat you? I don't believe anything you ever say to me." Mom despised herself, but she despised me even more, because I reminded her of what she could have become. She was determined to never let me forget how she felt about me. She told me, "You make me sick and I hate to see your black ass coming".

Even though I knew I was not fat, I still spent many hours playing basketball, exercising and working out trying to appease mom, but it never worked. Because I worked out so much I would come home starving and needing to eat, she would say, "Faye I hate you and I don't care if you starve to death and never eat". As her alcoholism took over, she stopped cooking for the family altogether. She tried to control every move

I made. She despised us so much she would not allow us to cook, "her food". She said, "You all don't own anything and all the food belong to me. If I say you all can eat, you can eat and if I say you can't eat then you cannot." On the rare occasions when she went to the store alone, she would only buy junk food and sweets, because that's what her body craved. Even with the sweets, my favorites at that time, we were not allowed to eat them without her strict permission. In spite of our very limited food consumption, she was convinced that we ate too much food. She made fun of us not having a lot of food to eat. She was mean and selfish and always called me botly (fat). She sat and guarded that kitchen like a military soldier on guard duty.

Chapter IX– Soundtracks of My Childhood

The soundtracks of my childhood were driven by whatever emotions mom was experiencing. Her moods swung from cold to hot to volcanic in a matter of seconds. Her sadness, depression, isolation, emptiness, rage, anger, bitterness and others determined which of her many favorite artists she demanded us to play. Some of her favorites included Sam Cooke, Aretha Franklin, Diana Ross and Supremes, Gladys Knight and the Pips, Smokey Robinson and the Miracles, Little Anthony and the Imperials, The Platters, Al Green, Donna Summers, McKinley Mitchell, BB King, Johnny Taylor and many more.

When she was very hurt by one of her many lovers she played Aretha Franklin, Al Green or Gladys Knight and the Pips. During the "family gatherings" she demanded Johnny Taylor, McKinley Mitchell or BB King. Family gatherings were gatherings of my family in the early 1970's when they would play music, drink alcohol, remember the good ole days and fight each other. When she was in a party mood she demanded Donna Summers or Diana Ross. When she was sad, crying, and angry over her father she only demanded Sam Cooke. On some Sunday mornings she demanded Sam Cook and the Soul Stirrers. These artist spent more time in my home than any family or friends. Their songs played so much I felt like I knew the artist. Mom loved music; she requested that we play music from sun up until sun down, especially sad music. She never grew tired of music, no matter how intoxicated she was. I think music drowned out the voices in her head some times.

One morning at 2am, she is on one of her drunken binges and she wanted to hear Sam Cook. We told her it is 2am and begged her to let us sleep, because we had school in a few hours. But she ignored our begging and she continued to demand, "I want to hear Sam Cook"! She had no value for education. She would say, "I have a second grade education and I turned out alright. You all don't have to go to school". I knew if I was going to be successful, I was going to have to ignore her negativity and push through to become successful. She never had any respect for us going to school or for us needing rest for school. She continued to demand for us to play Sam Cook. Her addictions drove her life and our lives. She only cared about getting intoxicated. Whenever she was on a drunken binge she was in her own "time zone".

She was the kind of alcoholic that drank until the stores and liquor stores ran out of alcohol or she blacked out, whichever came first.

Like every day she fed her sadness and depression with alcohol, prescription medication and sad music. She repeatedly demanded, "Okay Faye, play Sam Cooke, play Sam Cooke, play Sam Cooke", over and over and over again until day light hit. When I was a kid we had a manual stereo system that you had to stop and start and repeat and rewind. This is why we were forced to stay up all night long repeating one song on the stereo system over and over again. She was the most selfish person I have ever met; nothing mattered but what she wanted and whatever she wanted to do she did it. Nothing mattered but the music. Sleep deprivation, sad music, alcohol mixed with prescription medication, depression, sadness and isolation led her to do countless dangerous things, including boil pots of hot water and burn me. The night and morning after "The Burn", she still demanded that I play her music. The one Sam Cook song that she demanded the most was, "A Change is Gonna Come". Her favorite lyrics were, "It is too hard living, but I am afraid to die, because I don't know what is up there in the sky". She was obsessed with this part of the song. She demanded that I get up and play it over and over and over again. Because she was intoxicated every hour of every day, she did not have any real sense of the time of day. Her demands were not limited to music. She often demanded that I clean the house and go to the corner store and get her some alcohol and cigarettes. After I had done everything she wanted me to do she would order, "Play me some music". This started as soon as I walked into the house from school and went on until the next morning when it was time to go to school again. She did not allow me to sleep during the night, so I drifted off to sleep in between each song, which was the only way I was going to get any sleep. I was never fully functional in school. I could never focus, study and learn in school, because I was up all night meeting her demands. I told her how difficult it was for me to focus in school, study at home and learn. I told her that she was forcing me to stay up all night playing her music. She never listened to me nor did she care about how her destructive behaviors were hurting me. As a matter of fact, I believe she took some pleasure in all the difficulty she brought to my life. The reality was that she was a diseased addict, who was compulsive, impulse driven and out-of-control. The only thing mom seem to ever want to do was listen to music, drink alcohol, get intoxicated, party and cry all day and night, but all without any interruption. Mom believed that my real purpose was to serve her; take care of my siblings; clean her house; go to the corner store to purchase her alcohol and cigarettes; and to do everything else she demanded and ordered me to do. When I had done all these things for her; she cursed, tortured and abused me. She repeatedly made it clear to me that I was just getting in her way.

Whenever Sam Cooke was not the demand, another spirit, mood and emotion would come over her. Aretha Franklin's "Chain of Fools", was the second runner up to Sam Cooke. We paid for her being somebodies chain of fool. She was an addict who was an insomniac and her emotions swung from hatred, bitterness, sadness, loneliness, depression to self-pity. She drank until her body collapsed under the pressure of alcohol, prescription medication and lack of sleep.

Other times she would binge for days at a time.

During these times she would say, "I hate you, Faye, I

will kill you and call you". There were days and nights

I was so tired that I made the mistake of falling asleep

and did not repeat the music. She would wake me up

by yelling and cursing saying, "You black whore, if

you don't put that music back on, I will kill you, Faye".

Some days I absolutely hated her, but other days I

loved and pitied her. There were a few nights I

managed to get some sleep. Because I ran and hid

from her in one of the bedrooms, locked the door, and

push the bunk beds behind the door for safety. We

knew from past experiences that if we did not lock our

bedroom doors, she would come inside and hurt us.

When she could not find me to play her music, she

became very angry. She would get up out of her

chair, come out of the kitchen and search the entire

house for me so I could play her music. If she left the

kitchen and searched the house this was a huge deal. Because normally the only time she left that kitchen was to go to the bathroom, give orders and for the hours of torture. So I knew she was angry at me and wanted to hurt me. She came to the bedroom door with a knife in her hand and began stabbing the door with the knife. Yelling and cursing, "Faye, you black bitch, I know you are in there hiding. You better come out and play my music or it will be hell to pay". I would not come out because I was safer behind closed doors. I knew she was going to get me much worse if I had come out. In her search for me, she repeatedly passed by the stereo, but she was so stubborn and controlling that she never stop to play her own music. Maybe it did occur to her, but she did not want to do it, because she preferred to harass me. No matter how much we did for her, she was never satisfied. She did not just listen to her music and be quiet. All night long she would get more and more enraged as she listened to the music. It was as if she used the music to pump herself up to hurt me. The music did not sooth or calm, but those sad songs brought out great rage in her. As she listened to "A Change is Gonna Come", she would yell and cry out, "when is my change coming?" When she heard Aretha Franklin's song, "Chain of Fools" she became mad at every man in the world, including her eight sons. After a long day or night of torture she started all over again with her demands, "Faye, get up, pour me a glass of beer, light me a cigarette, put my music on and clean this house." Intoxicated or not she required me to do it in the order she demanded. Whenever I did not do it exactly as she ordered, she became very angry, cursed at me and tried to hurt me.

Mom controlled everything and everyone in my life; even my love and passion for basketball. The way she loved music and alcohol, is the way I loved basketball. I had a great love and passion for basketball. I loved everything about basketball and could not wait to play it in high school. But because she was jealous of anything I focused on other than her, I was not allowed to stay and play basketball in high school. The music was sad, but mom and our home were sadder. I heard Sam Cooke's song "A Change is Gonna Come", at least a billion. I rehearsed the lyrics repeatedly, "it is too hard living, but I am afraid to die, because I don't know what is up there beyond the sky". It was not until recent months that I could listen to Sam Cooke and Aretha Franklin without getting depressed. These songs triggered such sad emotions within me which made these songs so difficult for me. Because these songs were playing while I was tortured and abused, it has been very difficult to hear them.

God always gave me a "smile", in spite of mom. I managed to maintain the appearance of joy in the face of the thunder and lightning going on inside and outside of me. She tried to destroy my smile by saying, "Faye, you have a black and ugly face, red lips, white teeth and you smile like a fool". She continued, "I hate your smile, what do you have to smile about"? I still told myself, "There is something better in life other than what I am experiencing with my mom". In 1977, my aunt Darling drank herself to death. Her death was so devastating to mom. At the time of Aunt Darling's death, mom was addicted to McKinley Mitchell's song "End of a Rainbow". She literally played it billions of times. The lyrics, "I went running to the end of a rainbow, looking for the treasure they said I would find, but I found nothing but heartaches and trouble'. She treated this song as if it was the theme song or sound-track to her life. Mom said, "I want to die with my sister, Darling and I want to be with my mom". After Aunt Darling's death, she spent a larger amount of time fixated on death and longing to die. She made us play "End of a Rainbow", and then said, "Go refill my glass and light me a cigarette". She nursed, cursed, and rehearsed her pain over and over again. She said, "My sister was the only one who loved me, now she is gone". Aunt Darling's death was one more reason for her to drink even more. The more she drank the less focused on parenting and just life in general. She isolated herself in the kitchen even more than before. After Aunt Darling's death it was very clear that she was sick of living and wanted to die. She said, "Y'all children are destroying my life and taking up all of my time". She gave up on living and she repeatedly said, "I am ready to die, I am going where my sister is". Her addictions increased and her obsession with death consumed her life.

About six months after the death of Aunt Darling, she settled back into her previous routines. Once again she listened to Aretha Franklin's "Chain of Fools" and shifted her focus back to her own broken heart. She had a beautiful voice and she sang behind the song, as she cried. In between singing she would cry out loud saying, "I was such a fool for my husband, JD, Sr. and he made such a fool out of me". In her intoxication, she said terrible things about him, so she felt completely betrayed and mistreated by him. Her father set the dysfunctional standard of love for her, and then she turned around and married JD, Sr. who was just like her father. My grandfather and JD, Sr. set the tone for the pain the rest of us paid for. Aretha Franklins, "Chain of Fools" was such a sad song to mom, because it reminded her of the love she gave to JD, but he did not return that love to her. Because she never healed from these two great loves, she was not much good for anyone else. She was so busy looking backward at these two destructive relationships that she could never move forward. She would cry and say, "That no good, dirty dog came back to see his kids, after he left us for six months. I am his wife; he had his mammie in the car with him. She was begging me to take him back. I hate him; I hate his mammie too". It was clear that her heart was broken, but she did not know how to channel all her pain, so she spent her life hurting others. She said, "A man ain't nothing but a dog" or "A man has got portions of a dog in him". She never got over the pain from her father or the pain of JD, Sr. Every day she nursed, rehearsed and cursed the agony of her past pains. She longed to die. She would say, "I wish I was dead", Lord, come and take

me", or "Lord I wish I was dead, just kill me right now".

It saddened, yet terrified me to see her in such a

tormented state. When mom was intoxicated her

eyes were blood shot red, her skin discolored and

bloody, her features were distorted, and she looked

demon possessed. When she was in this intoxicated

and demonic state, even if the music was playing in

the background, she focused her attention toward

torturing me and my siblings. The music seemed like

my enemy for many years, but it was not the music at

all, but the terrible events the occurred in my home,

while the music was being played. The music still

takes me back but things are different now, because I

am in control not the sad events from my past. The

soundtracks of my childhood still have powerful

influence in my life. I can hear a song that is played

and that song has the power to transform my mind to

a certain time and place. I can recall my memories surrounding that song, the smells in the room, even the smell of mom and exactly what she did and said to me.

Chapter X - Successfully Surviving the Monster

Today, I beat the odds. I am successfully surviving the monster, which was my mom. I am living proof that beating the odds is a process not an event. Every day I am taking this journey. I am determined and committed to be a successful survivor. I have three godly, educated, successful and well balanced young adult children. I have obtained a Bachelor's degree in Psychology and a Master's degree in Counseling. In spite of the monster I possess a peace from God that has passed all my understanding.

I am putting the pieces of my life together; while serving others and being the most productive person that I can be. Many people experience torture, abuse and pain even more than we as a society are willing to admit. As a successful survivor, I have a responsibility to reach out and help victims and survivors to become successful survivors. My greatest motivation for writing my story is to heal and become healthy. Second to my healing, is a strong desire to motivate, inspire and to empower others. Healthy and successful survivors must understand that the choice is ours; not our abusers. I understand now that each person is the sum total of his or her life experiences. Each person is accountable and responsible for how they use or abuse those experiences.

Every parent and every person must ask the important questions. How did my childhood and life experiences shape me? Did my parents honestly do their best? Did my parents do what they knew? Did my parents learn new and better behaviors? Did my parents simply do to me, what was done to them? What am I going to do? Am I going to repeat the same patterns? Am I going to break the cycle? What am I doing?

Despite mom's cruel, empty, present yet absent and abusive behaviors; I broke my family cycle. Every day I make the conscious decision to be a successful survivor. I decided that my three children (Isaiah, Daniel and Carolyn) and anyone else I could help deserved my best. They deserved more from me than I received from my monster. Mom survived her childhood abuse, but she used her life to repeat the same family legacy of destructiveness. She showed me that there is a difference between survivors and successful survivors; survivors live through their abuse. Successful survivors use their success to inspire, motivate and empower other to become successful.

I have worked really hard and have chosen to make my life a triumphant victory, not a tragedy. I am kind to others and I love as hard as I can. I am always present in every relationship; so that people will always know that they have been touched and loved by me. I live to inspire as many people as I can to be the best person they can be. Mom was a monster; I have made the decision to be like God and to love others in spite of the way they love or treat me. Today, I am not that helpless child who could not fight back, but I am a successful survivor who is fighting back through every positive channel that I can. Every experience, good or bad has served a great purpose in my life. I understand that I have a choice. I choose not to repeat the family legacy, but to change my horrific family legacy and create a new one. Each day I make a conscious decision to build up and not to destroy.

Since I started writing this story, there were many nights I either couldn't sleep or I would have nightmares, which would completely exhaust me. There are some days I am in so much pain dealing with past pain that it feels like someone is cutting my heart out of my chest, but I am awake feeling all the pain. Other times I tell myself that I had put enough time and space between my present and my past and I can write this story without dealing with so much pain. Before I know it, I am back in pain again.

Every day is a challenge for me to deal with my pain; but I push through to get on the other side of my pain.

Until recently I did not have the courage to deal with so many unresolved issues, feelings, emotions. Now I know the only way to get through is to emotionally go back, walk through the mine fields of my past pain and then slowly walk forward. I thought if I opened up too much of my past pain, I would not be a fit parent or person. But the truth is, since I started writing, remembering and re-living my past, I have been able to successfully and appropriately deal with my past.

Today, I know what mom did not know; our past pain is only as big and dangerous as we allow it to be. When I deal with this pain prayerfully and appropriately, I grow and place myself in a position and space to be able to help others. I have decided that it is time for me to deal with my past head on. I am making peace with each event from my past that I had no control and power over. I had to understand and admit that it was not my fault that mom was abusive and unable to love. I made the decision to break my family legacy and the cycle of abuse, alcohol and drug addiction, and family dysfunction. I admitted all these problems existed in my family and then I committed to break those cycles. I have equipped and educated myself by learning new strategies (knowledge and behaviors) that could replace the old destructive family patterns. I began to practice and live by this new information. Now, I am prayerfully living a successful and productive life. It still hurts, but I am now able to deal with the hurt and use that hurt to help others live a successful and productive life. My hurt, pain and anguish motivated me to go through the healing process and now I can help others to heal.

For me, the hardest challenge of growing up with an alcoholic, torturous, abusive, cruel, and insensitive mother was not surviving, but not repeating the same behavior with my three amazing children. Even with new knowledge and behavior I still feared that I would become the monster that was my mother. I have worked and am working very hard not to allow the negativity of my childhood to define me. God blessed me with wisdom, self-control, and the book (Bible) of love and life to guide me as I parented my children. I have allowed my past to motivate me to be a better person. My daily challenge is not allowing those moments of abuse, cruelty and torture to define the rest of my life.